CW00732806

the technique of POTTERY

the technique of POTTERY

Dora Billington
revised by
John Colbeck

B T Batsford Limited
London and Sydney

This edition first published 1974
ISBN 0 7134 2836 8

Designed by Charlotte Gerlings, Libra Studios
Filmset in Monophoto Baskerville (169)
10 on 12 point by Tradespools Ltd
Frome, Somerset
Printed in Great Britain by
Butler & Tanner Ltd, Frome, Somerset
for the publishers
B T Batsford Limited
4 Fitzhardinge Street, London W1H 0AH and
23 Cross Street, PO Box 586
Brookvale, NSW 2100

Acknowledgment

I am grateful to the British Museum and Victoria and Albert Museum for permission to reproduce photographs of pottery in their collections.

I am grateful to Mrs M Bird and Mrs H P Hobbs for typing the manuscript with speed and care.

My especial thanks are due to Thelma M Nye for her patience and for her advice at all stages of this revision; to Bonnie van de Wetering for taking all the photographs of demonstrations in Section Two with patience and understanding; and to Gilbert Harding-Green, who knew Dora Billington as a friend and worked with her as a colleague for over thirty years, for various conversations about Dora Billington's teaching of and attitudes to pottery.

John Colbeck 1974

Contents

Introduction to first edition

Pottery is a unique and exciting craft; it ranges from the purely aesthetic to the purely functional; in scope from the architectural wall covering to the small and exquisite cup and saucer or statuette. Coarse or fine, large or small, glazed or unglazed, pottery fulfils many functions and reveals at every turn a new beauty, while remaining of the earth, earthy.

Primarily sculptural – the shape must of necessity come first – pottery can and does at one time or another employ to clothe its surfaces every kind of graphic art; at least it is difficult to imagine one that could not be if it has not already been, used. Today more than ever before the field is wide open to experiment; there is a new freedom. Try anything; all the old rules are open to question, though that is not to say that they will be found invalid; but it does mean that every potter can now make whatever kind of pottery he pleases, and that he alone is responsible. No longer can he lean back on a comfortable tradition, however good. Neither is it necessary to spurn all tradition in order to be modern; that is as reprehensible as wilful ignorance. But, through constant enquiry and experiment, with ever-increasing sureness and sensibility, he must satisfy himself as to what is good, or at any rate relevant to the particular work he wants to do.

The traditional peasant potter, using the materials that were at hand, developing very slowly the craft he had inherited, and knowing only one kind of pottery made according to well-proven and time-honoured methods, made pots which had a logical directness and usually a real if largely unconscious beauty.

Then came the factory with its division of labour, bringing in from outside the craft influences of many kinds as well as new materials and new methods, and substituting for the simple if sometimes crude beauty of the old traditional wares other and more sophisticated standards, good, bad and indifferent.

But just as the peasant potter was at the point of

extinction, in Britain at least, the craft revival of the late nineteenth century brought a new interest in and a new appraisal of his wares; and not without a certain wry humour did he see his traditional skill quickly acquired by a new and enthusiastic type of craftsman, the self-conscious 'artist potter', or, to use a less challenging term, the 'studio potter', soon to be established in considerable numbers.

The studio potter of today is not and cannot be just a peasant potter; books, museums, travel, have brought to his notice the pottery of all ages and places, widening his knowledge and experience, and bringing also the eclecticism inescapable to our generation. No longer are the established standards accepted without question; the potter must think as clearly as he can about the thing he wants to make; he must have the courage, and the honesty, to make it in the best way he can without any faking, and the result must justify itself. To have so many techniques all waiting to be tried, so much available information, and so many examples to follow is very exciting, even a little heady, and the student should feel free to try anything, even the most unorthodox methods: in time he must and will decide what he most wants to make and how best to make it, according to his ability and working conditions, and thus in time he will create his own 'style'.

And although it is conceivable, even probable, that pottery for everyday use will be superseded by some form of plastic it is quite inconceivable that it will ever cease to be made and become something of merely archaeological and antiquarian interest. We cannot foresee the taste and appreciation of future generations, but, as far as we *can* see, the peculiar qualities of usefulness and beauty of pottery would seem to ensure its place in the affection of all those who care about things; not only of the past, but things of beauty to use. And at present there are plenty of people eager to work hard for little reward, except the joy of making beautiful pots.

Dora Billington Spring 1962

Introduction to revised edition

The need for a revision of any book can arise from two main reasons: the book may be about a subject which is changing and may therefore need factual revisions and additions to bring it up to date or it may be about a relatively unchanging subject and require revision because the processes and fashions of book production have changed. The need for revision in the case of Dora Billington's *The Technique of Pottery* is in the latter category. But there is an additional reason because Dora Billington through quite extraordinary willpower and perseverance began and completed her book after she had suffered a severe and permanently paralysing stroke. She was disappointed that she was unable to illustrate the sections on making and decorating more fully.

My aim therefore in revising *The Technique of Pottery* was both to try to fulfil the publishers brief and also to try to do what Dora Billington would have liked, but was unable to do. That people should understand the principles, possibilities and distinct qualities of the different making and decorating processes was central to the teaching of Dora Billington so to this end Section Two of the revised edition dealing with making processes is illustrated mainly with photographs of demonstrations of technique and Section Four describing decorating processes is illustrated with various traditional examples. In many cases these illustrations directly replace textual sections in the original edition.

The brief to revise *The Technique of Pottery* was a specific one. I was asked to reillustrate the book, to rewrite and reorganise it as seemed necessary and to simplify it where seemed appropriate. It is therefore a major revision. The rewriting which has occurred was necessitated mainly by the re-illustration and partly by some simplifications. The major simplifications are the omitting of the detailed descriptions of fairly complex mould making for slip casting and of the jigger and jolley process – both these processes are still described but at a simpler level emphasising first principles which brings these descriptions more in line with those of other sections. The reorganisation which has occurred is relatively slight and is intended to group the content into larger simpler sections than occurred in the separate chapters of the original edition. Though the appearance and order of the book are considerably changed I have made every effort to retain the original content and most importantly the original emphases.

Two main emphases and a third related one emerge from Dora Billington's book. The first concerns the exciting breadth of the field of pottery. The second concerns the responsibility of the individual to know this breadth and to experiment within it to evolve personal attitudes and interests from experience. The third related emphasis is the new relevance of the past and the foreign traditions of which craftsmen and artists of the past were often inevitably ignorant – this not as a prop for ideas but as an experience of the breadth of process and quality available. It is because I am in total sympathy with these emphases that I undertook the present revision.

Individual craftsmen-potters or artist-potters, call them what you wish, had virtually ceased to exist by the end of the first quarter of the nineteenth century and fast diminished long before that. The crafts which survived were only those relevant to the industrial situation and even these became increasingly more mechanised. When the craft revival began in the last quarter of the nineteenth century and as it continued in the first quarter of the twentieth century some attempt was made to pick up the threads where they had been left but the world was changed. Travel, museums and books had made people more aware of past and foreign traditions and processes and the new 'artist potters' experimented with and used a wide range of processes and qualities. It is a sadness that in the second quarter of the twentieth century this breadth of experiment diminished. One figure who emerged in this period above all others was Bernard Leach. His lasting concern after other initial experiments was with one of the many foreign traditions of which people had become aware, that of oriental stoneware and porcelain. It is a sadness that there were not other people working at that time of comparable stature, understanding and sincerity but with different interests.

That since the war there has been a broadening of interest in the scope of pottery is due in no small measure to the teaching of Dora Billington at the Central School of Arts and Crafts, as it then was. She pioneered and prophesied this revival of interest, she pointed to the need to experience the range of materials and qualities both through first hand experience and through a study of history:

> 'What is worth considering in these days of hurried eclecticism is the rightness of the traditional forms of decoration: the smooth liquid quality of lead-glazed slipware, the crisp reliefs on salt glazed stoneware, the free painting on maiolica and faïence, the calligraphic brushwork on Chinese stoneware, or the pictorial engravings on English earthenware; each in its own way is so right, so suitable as to appear inevitable. Which in a way it was. The old potters knew their own materials and no others, and learnt to use them as they felt they ought to be used, and by degrees a tradition was established, only spoiled when inherited skill became conscious of its own cleverness. The position today is quite different: we can now, through museums and books, review the whole range of pottery and its development, we can know it, place it in its period, appreciate it up to a point, but this is inclined to give us a sense of frustration, of satiety: everything has been done, so what is there left to do? It is greatly to the credit of the younger potters that they have given their own interpretation to some of these methods, and are using old techniques to produce things in the idiom of today. They are no longer content with pastiche.'

She warned of the dangers of eclecticism:

> 'So much of our attempt at decoration in the Chinese manner meant nothing in itself nor did anything to help the pot.'

She stressed the need for each person to set his own criteria and accept responsibility:

> 'Today more than ever before the field is wide open to experiment; there is a new freedom. Try anything; all the old rules are open to question, though that is not to say that they will be found invalid; but it does mean that every potter can now make whatever kind of pottery he pleases, and that he alone is responsible. No longer can he lean back on a comfortable tradition, however good. Neither is it necessary to spurn all tradition in order to be modern; that is as reprehensible as wilful ignorance. But, through constant en-

quiry and experiment, with ever-increasing sureness and sensibility, he must satisfy himself as to what is good, or at any rate relevant to the particular work he wants to do.
'To have so many examples to follow is very exciting, even a little heady, and the student should feel free to try anything, even the most unorthodox methods: in time he must and will decide what he most wants to make and how best to make it, according to his ability and working conditions, and thus in time he will create his own "style".'
Pottery is a broad and complex craft which too often leads to over-technical attitudes which can obscure the exciting range of possibilities which exists. The dilemma is that for the possibilities to be realised the processes and materials have to be known and understood. Something of what Dora Billington worked for has been achieved. There is still more to achieve.

John Colbeck 1974

Section One Introduction

WHAT IS POTTERY

The term *pottery*, or *ceramics*, covers all objects made of clay, with or without the addition of other earthy materials, shaped first, dried, and then made hard and permanent by the action of the considerable heat of the potter's kiln. It is this application of heat that changes clay into pottery. Sunbaked clay may be dry and very hard but soaked in water it will always return to a soft plastic state. Once subjected to a temperature of red heat at least, and ranging up to 1350°C and more, certain chemical and physical changes take place which are not reversible – the clay can never again return to its plastic state.

Pottery is made from certain igneous (fire-formed) rocks and their residues after they have been naturally decomposed by water and carbon dioxide. The potter collects these materials, sorts and selects them, forms them and finally subjects them to heat and in doing all this recreates something of the nature of the original rocks. Pottery is really a fire-formed artificial stone and it is, generally speaking, as dense and indestructible as many rocks. It is, of course, brittle and easily smashed (as indeed are many rocks), but it cannot be destroyed by natural means. It is this permanence which makes pottery shards so valuable to the archaeologist as these survive when most other remains of ancient cultures (and more recent ones too) have long since vanished or deteriorated beyond recognition.

The layman tends to think of pottery as consisting mostly of clay shapes with a covering of glass, or *glaze*, but it was not always so and some kinds of pottery are still made which are not glazed. In classifying pottery the glaze, however, is incidental. The essential differences concern the clay, or *body*, and the heat to which it has been subjected.

There is some disagreement about classification of pottery but it is only an academic disagreement. Some authorities recognise only two classifications: soft pottery (earthenware) and hard pottery (stoneware and porcelain). Others recognise three: earthenware, stoneware and porcelain. Whether porcelain and stoneware are thought of separately or as being subdivisions of one type is not important. It should be added that whether two or three classifications are recognised there is a range of qualities evident in each and the divisions between the categories are indistinct in many particular cases. The differences between the main types are physical.

Earthenware is soft. It can be scratched with a knife. It is opaque and porous, and fractures granularly. The suction in a piece of unglazed earthenware held against the tongue can be felt. If a broken section of glazed earthenware is examined the glaze will be seen to be quite distinct from the body.

Stoneware is hard. It cannot be scratched with a knife. It is opaque and non porous, and fractures vitreously. If a piece of unglazed stoneware is held against the tongue no suction can be felt. If a broken section of glazed stoneware is examined the glaze will be seen to merge almost imperceptibly into the vitreous body. It is denser than earthenware.

Porcelain is hard. It cannot be scratched with a knife. It is non porous. It is denser than earthenware. If a piece of unglazed porcelain is held against the tongue no suction can be felt. In porcelain there is the closest union of glaze and body which can be seen if a broken section is examined. Porcelain has a vitreous and often conchoidal fracture. Porcelain is translucent. Its translucency distinguishes it from earthenware and stoneware. Though obviously there are limits, the translucency of porcelain is not dependent on extreme thinness. This quality of translucency is easy to check: when porcelain, thin or quite thick, is held up to the light the shadows of fingers moving behind the piece will be clearly visible.

Within each category a wide range of qualities can be found. Some industrial bodies such as bone china or vitreous earthenware are difficult to classify clearly in one section or another. But for most pottery these main classifications are a useful starting point.

The differences of the materials present in these main classifications and in the many subdivisions within them are surprisingly small. All these different kinds of pottery arise from the use and mixture of different kinds of naturally occurring clays and other materials. The differences between these clays and materials are chemically relatively slight but the distinct varieties they can produce and have produced are infinite.

CLAY AND POTTERY BODIES

The one indispensable ingredient of all pottery is clay. Clay is the product of the disintegration and decomposition of granitic and fel(d)spathic rocks. These rocks are of volcanic origin and are composed of fel(d)spar, crystalline silica, mica and other silicious compounds. When exposed on the earth's surface these rocks very, very slowly disintegrate and decompose through the action of water, frost and carbonic acid (this latter from the humus in the surface soil and vegetation).

The formation of clay

Granite (or cornish or china stone as it is known to potters) is a granular rock composed of quartz (a crystalline form of silica), felspar (a combination of potash (and/or sometimes soda) alumina and silica) and a small amount of mica (a substance rather like felspar in composition but with a different structure).

The decomposition of granitic rocks can be expressed simply and arbitrarily as:

$$\underbrace{K_2OAl_2O_36SiO_2}_{\text{felspar}} + H_2O + CO_2 =$$

$$\underbrace{Al_2O_32SiO_22H_2O}_{\text{clay}} + K_2CO_3 + SiO_2$$

Subjected to the attack of water and carbonic acid the rock first loses its potash which is dissolved out by the carbon dioxide and water and escapes as potassium carbonate in solution. The felspar is thus broken down, the residues being clay, silica and a little mica. It is not, of course, as neat as this in practice and what is found consists of clay together with the debris of partially decomposed rock and disintegrated but undecomposed rock. The clay being the finest of the materials can be separated by flotation. Deposits are worked by playing water onto the mixed material and allowing the water and material to flow through separating pools into settling pools.

Classifications of clay

The clay thus formed and mined is known as primary or sedimentary clay. Potters call it china clay or kaolin. China clay, though very pure, is not very plastic. Its particle size is relatively coarse. Deposits of china clay are relatively scarce. In England commercially workable deposits are mainly confined to Cornwall.

Clays known as secondary clays are far commoner than primary clays. These are clays which have been transported by the action of rivers, lakes and seas at some stage in the vast span of geologic time from their beds of formation to new places, originally probably lakes, swamps, river beds or the sea bed, where they have been deposited. Deposits of secondary clays are extremely widely distributed – few areas of the world are very remote from beds of one variety or another of secondary clay.

During the process of transportation two important things happened to this clay. Firstly it accumulated additions both vegetable and mineral of various kinds. Secondly the attrition of movement broke down the coarse particles of the original primary clay to finer and finer particles. A characteristic, the important characteristic, of secondary clay is its plasticity, the quality which enables it to be readily formed into shapes and to retain those shapes.

There are three main types of secondary clays: refractory clays, vitrifiable clays and fusible clays.

Refractory clays are found in coal-bearing areas, sometimes actually between coal seams. These clays are often known as fireclays. They are used for making firebricks and other refractory goods. They can vary from being very fine to being very coarse. Being refractory and often of rich texture fireclays are frequently a constituent of stoneware bodies.

Vitrifiable clays vary greatly in nature and colour. Ball clay is a vitrifiable clay which has exceptional plasticity. It is an important constituent of both earthenware and stoneware bodies.

Fusible secondary clays (sometimes called tertiary clays) are surface clays and usually have a high proportion of iron oxide which has been picked up during their transportation from their beds of formation. Their common use is for building bricks and tiles and was for coarse wares such as flower pots and bread crocks.

Within the three classifications of secondary clays there is a very rich variety of clays of different textures, different colours and different working qualities. It is a mistake to be misled into trying to predict the fired colour of clay from its unfired colour. Much of the colour of secondary clays is due to the presence of decayed vegetable matter which stains the clay a variety of colours which disappear totally in the firing, for example many light firing ball clays are nearly black when dug. Iron oxide is the most common colouring agent in rocks and virtually all secondary clays contain iron oxide in greater or lesser amounts. Iron colouring of clays in their natural state is, of course, reflected in the fired colour of affected clays.

Preparation of clay for use

When clay has been dug it is generally left to weather for a year or two. This weathering allows it to be dried by the sun and broken down by rain and frost. When weathered it is dried and then broken up and mixed with water into a slip. It may then be sieved and is subsequently dried by one means or another and put through a pugmill ready for use.

It is perfectly possible and can be instructive to dig and prepare clay. But it can also be very frustrating unless it is certain that the particular clay is worthwhile. The clay in the garden is most likely to be a rather poor fusible secondary clay. A reliable vitrifiable secondary clay when subject under test to increasingly high temperatures will respond by gradually becoming less and less porous and more and more vitreous. A poor fusible clay subject under test to increasingly high temperatures will often respond by changing from being relatively porous to actually beginning to melt and this change can occur within a very small temperature range. The two first tests to determine whether a particular clay might be worth digging are a shrinkage test and the firing test. Tablets of clay are marked with measurements in the plastic state and these measurements are checked when the clay is dry. If this shrinkage is more than one in six it is too great and the clay should be forgotten. If it passes the shrinkage test then tablets should be test fired at ever increasing temperatures to determine whether or not the clay is likely to bubble or boil or distort at reasonable working temperatures.

There is much to be said for spending time finding out about the varieties of clay which are available prepared rather than spending time digging, educational as this may be at a certain stage.

Additions to clay bodies

Any clay can be added to any other clay to achieve a blend of their working qualities but it should not be forgotten that this inevitably alters the firing qualities of the clay. Equally, blending to adjust the latter will affect the working qualities of a clay.

Materials other than clay can be added to bodies to change their colour, texture, fusibility or refractoriness.

Flint prepared by calcining and grinding till very fine, is practically pure silica and can be added to give increased whiteness, density and refractoriness. It has no plasticity. Its use can increase rigidity and help to prevent warping. An excessive use of flint can make a body liable to cracking.

Silver sand is the cleanest of sands and it can be added to give texture and grip to clays which seem too smooth. Sand is almost pure silica so sand additions tend to make bodies more refractory. Great care should be exercised with sand of unknown origin and sand from builders' merchants or found sand and it should always be well tested. Sand may contain iron pyrites which can be troublesome and some sands may even tend to fuse at quite ordinary working temperatures.

Quartz is practically pure silica in crystalline form and it can be substituted for flint.

Grog is made by grinding up fired clay. It can be bought ground to a variety of finenesses. Its function in bodies is to give texture and to reduce shrinkage. Grog is usually made of refractory light firing clay but there is no reason why grog cannot be made of darker firing clays and used to give a colour texture to a body.

Cornish stone and *felspar* are used in bodies to promote fusion and thus to give hardness and density. Fired to an appropriate temperature and combined with china clay they produce translucent porcelain.

Bentonite is an exceptionally plastic ball clay. The addition of up to 5% of it will increase the plasticity of a body considerably without greatly altering other qualities.

Calcined animal bones provide calcium phosphate in English china bodies which acts as a flux making the body denser and, in conjunction with china stone or felspar, translucent.

The nature of plasticity

The plastic quality of clay is due to its structure. Clay particles are like thin flat scales. When lubricated with water these scales can slide over each other. When the water evaporates they close up and cannot move. When an excess of water is present the particles fall apart. A comparison which has been made and which can be enlightening is to take a number of small sheets of glass and to stack them up, wetting each one as it is placed on the next. The stack can be easily distorted sideways in any direction but cannot be pulled apart in a vertical direction. The comparison is good but limited in that with clay distortion in any direction, not just in one plane, is possible.

It is the finer particle size of secondary clays which allows the particles freer movement than is possible with the coarser particles of china clay. This is why secondary clays are the most plastic.

Machines of use in the mixing of bodies Industrially bodies are prepared in vast mixing machines called blungers in the slip state. The mixed slip has the water squeezed out of it under pressure in a filter press, which produces flat sheets of plastic clay from the mixed slip.

This heavy machinery is rarely available in contexts other than the industry.

Mixing by hand Bodies can be mixed by hand from powdered ingredients in bins. The powdered material is always added to the water and if large amounts are being mixed the materials should be added in rotation in proportionate amounts to facilitate mixing. When thoroughly mixed the mixture is dried out on plaster or *Asbestolux*. This certainly is hard work but clays of excellent, specific qualities can be mixed and in some circumstances the extra work is worthwhile. (Much better stoneware throwing clays, for example, can be mixed from ball clay and fireclay powder than can be bought ready mixed in a plastic state.)

The maintenance and reclamation of stocks of clay

Provided it is not allowed to dry out clay can be used over and over again (and when it has dried out it can, of course, be reclaimed for further use). Occasionally, especially if it has been repeatedly thrown, clay can get tired. When this occurs it should be 'rested', not used, for a week or so and then be wedged and kneaded for use when it will have ceased to be tired. It is a good idea to mix tired clay that has been rested with new clay. Part of the tiredness of throwing clay can be due to the loss of some of the finer particles of clay (which contribute greatly to plasticity) in slip during throwing. In general, however, clay improves through use.

Clay which has been thrown and is too soft for immediate re-use should not be thrown into a bin with clays of differing consistency to be reclaimed but should be put on one side to harden a little and then should be re-kneaded ready for use. This saves time and effort because the clay is basically even in consistency, having already been kneaded prior to throwing – though of course the clay will need preparation by kneading but this is very much easier than preparing clay, even pugged clay, from a reclaim bin containing a mixture of clays of varying consistencies.

Prepared plastic clay can be kept in condition very simply by being wrapped in sheets of polythene. Where the clay is in pugged lengths and presents therefore a larger surface area for air drying it is a good idea to cover the clay with damp sacking and to cover this with polythene.

The only clay which should need time consuming reclamation is the slurry from throwing wheels, which is valuable for its plasticity, and should be added to the water in reclamation bins, and clay which has become too dry to use. Leather-hard clay should not be put into reclaim bins but should be allowed to dry out completely. Dry clay, broken into reasonable sized pieces (and not too thick), breaks down completely and quickly when placed in water. It should be added to a bin of water gradually so it can be broken down by water without being surrounded by other broken down clay which inhibits the access of water. If the clay is broken down like this it will be far easier to wedge and knead effectively when it has been dried out (and perhaps pugged). When dry clay, leather-hard clay, plastic clay, slip and water are all mixed together in a bin, the unevennesses which exist will continue to do so right through the reclamation process (even with one or two puggings) and can only be removed by thorough wedging and kneading. If dry clay is gradually added to a bin of water and is stirred and mixed occasionally the resulting mixture will be basically even and far easier to prepare for use.

Wedging and kneading

Most clay that is bought in a plastic state will have been finally prepared by being passed through a pugmill. Pugmills de-air and mix clays quite thoroughly but through time and transportation prepared clays are rarely even when they reach their destination. Even if a pugmill is available the final preparation of the clay, especially for throwing, where its condition is perhaps most critically important, is better and, with practice, more quickly done by hand.

All the manual clay preparation processes require a firm table or bench. This should not be too high. If, when standing, the palms of one's hands just rest on the top then the maximum amount of weight can be exerted on the clay with the minimum of effort. The surface on which preparation is done should be reasonably smooth and slightly porous. Slate or marble set on a concrete bench are good. Concrete itself when floated to a really smooth finish is good. A solid timber table is perfectly adequate. Timber faced with marine ply or a good quality unsealed non-glossy lino is good. Some individuals use benches topped with a 76 mm to 102 mm plaster slab. Plaster offers the advantage of having an adjustable porosity. If the plaster is undampened the clay can be dried to a firmer condition as it is being prepared. If dampened it need have very little stiffening effect. Though it has these advantages, in the context of heavy use by a number of people it is not a good alternative – firstly its condition is unlikely ever to be what the next person needs and is likely to be permanently on the damp side and secondly with heavy use by a number of people the chances of mechanical damage are greater and plaster will all too easily begin to find its way into the clay.

Making the clay of even consistency and de-airing it are only two aspects of clay preparation. The third and very important one is giving it the right degree of softness for the work in hand. On the whole it is far easier and quicker to stiffen clay than to soften it. For this reason it is usual and much better to keep stocks of clay rather damper than the consistency likely to be required. Soft clay can be made firmer fairly quickly by squeezing large handfuls into rolls of about 38 mm to 50 mm diameter and about 203 mm long and then bending these into semi-circular arches and standing them on boards. In front of a fan (which is better if it is simply blowing air not heated air) these will stiffen up quite quickly or if such possibility exists they can be placed outside when, on any but the stillest of days, the clay will soon be firmer. Alternatively the soft clay can be spread out on *Asbestolux* boards or plaster slabs. *Asbestolux* has the disadvantage that it is not very strong but it has a good porosity and can be easily and quickly dried if it becomes very wet. Plaster has its usual disadvantage of accidental mechanical damage but does, when dry, stiffen clay very quickly. Slabs of plaster used for drying clay should be small enough to be readily portable so they can be conveniently moved to a heated or airy spot to be dried out.

When the clay is of approximately the right consistency it can be finally prepared by any of three methods or very often a combination of these.

Wedging Clay can be completely prepared by the process of wedging described below but more often it is used as a preparation for one or other of the types of kneading. It very quickly, and perhaps more easily than kneading evenly distributes unevennesses in a lump of clay. For this reason it is a frequent practice to wedge clay that has been stiffened up on *asbestolux* or plaster.

1 A reasonably large amount of clay but not more than can be easily handled is knocked into shape by banging on the table or pressing with the hands. The front end is eased off the table and a wire passed through from the bottom cutting the clay into two equal halves.

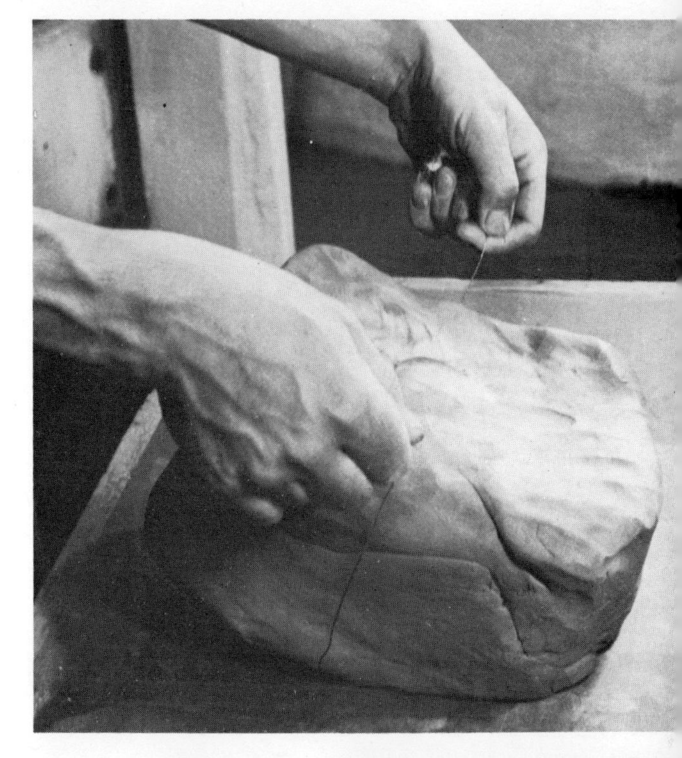

2 The loose front piece is picked up and as it is raised it is turned over so the cut surface faces the wedger and what was the top faces downwards.

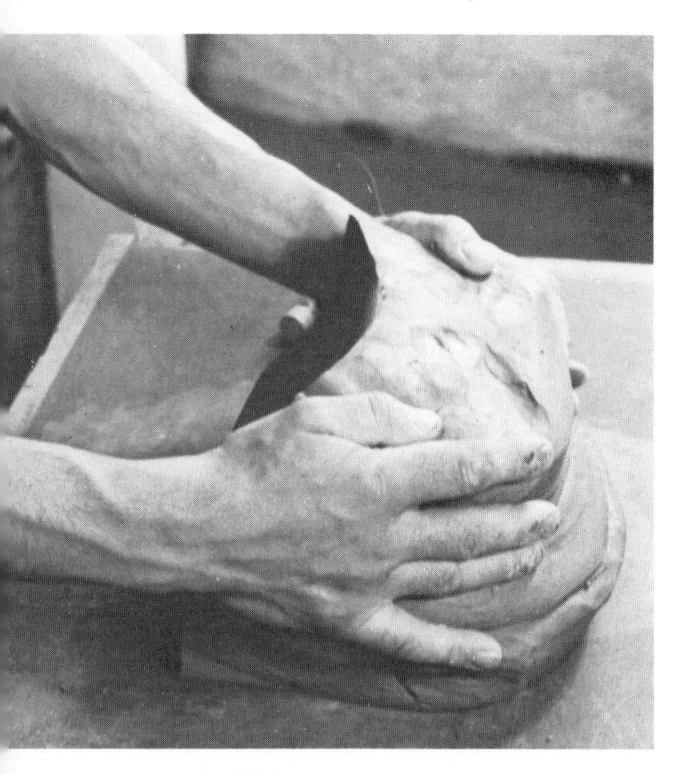

3 The piece is firmly thrown down on to the other half of the clay so that the two cut faces as nearly as possible coincide. The top of the new piece of clay is now what was the bottom of the original piece and the middle of the new piece is what was the top of the original.

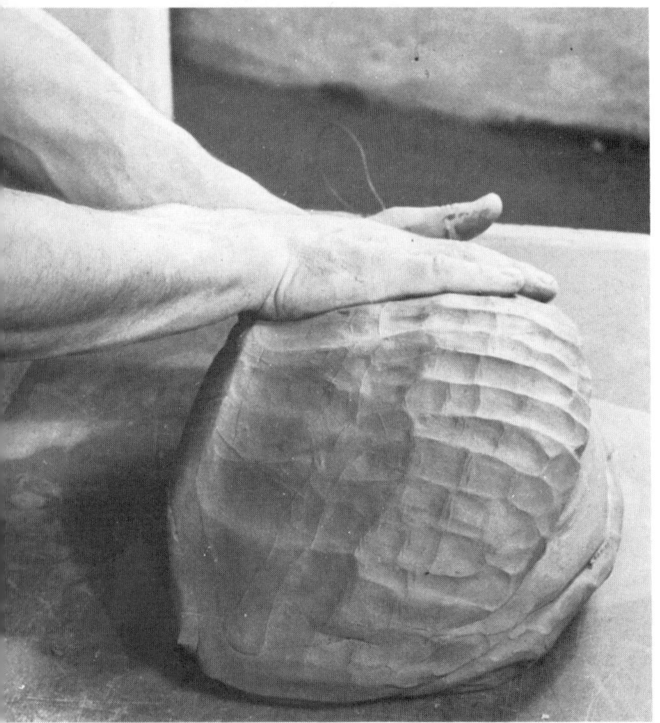

4 After the pieces have been thrown together the two edges and the back should be firmly tapped to close up folds.

5 After tapping the clay is freed from the bench, turned through 90° and dropped on to the table with the hands keeping the front end off the table.

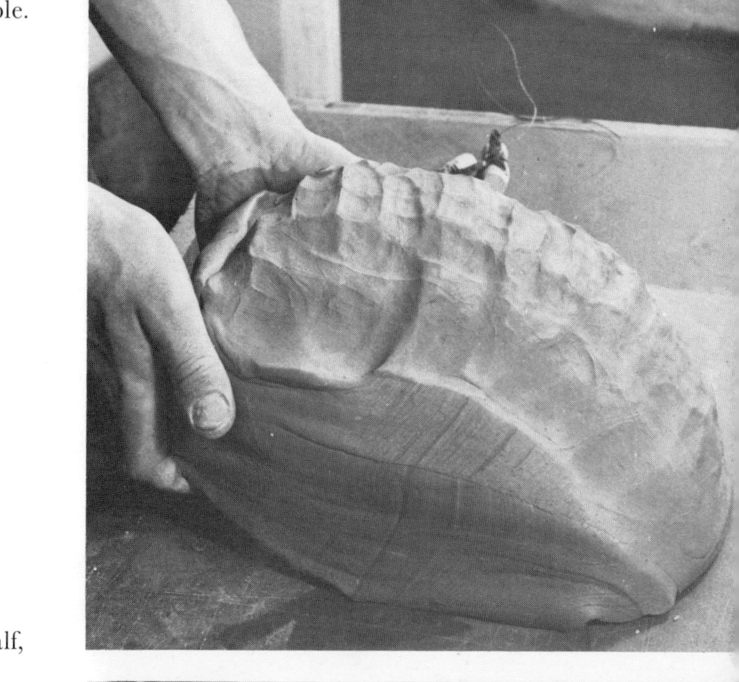

6 The wire is then passed under the raised half, the clay is cut, and the whole process repeated.

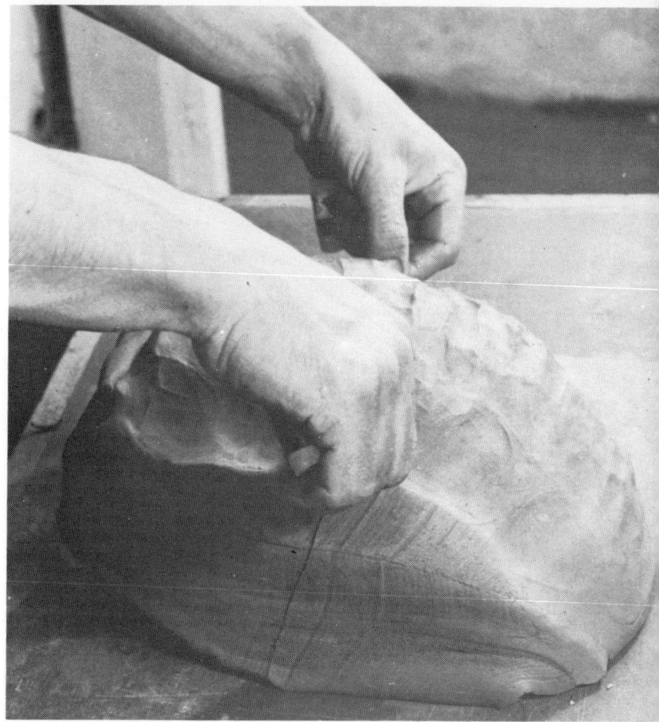

It will be seen that by this method unevenness is quickly distributed through the clay. If the process is continued the clay is made completely even. So that the spreading is not just in one plane the clay can be occasionally turned over through 90° as well as being turned round each time. When the two pieces have been thrown together if unevenness is present the force which the pressure of the throwing together has exerted throughout the piece can be seen in the cut surfaces which will be slightly rippled, see illustrations 5 and 6 above where the softer clay has been pushed out in convex folds further than the seams of firmer clay.

It is also possible to wedge clay on the edge of a table or bench by throwing it down half on and half off the bench and pushing through the clay with the hands on the edge of the table rather than cutting it with a wire.

A small piece of clay can be mixed by breaking it in half in the hands, turning the halves and throwing them together. Obviously this action is repeated a number of times.

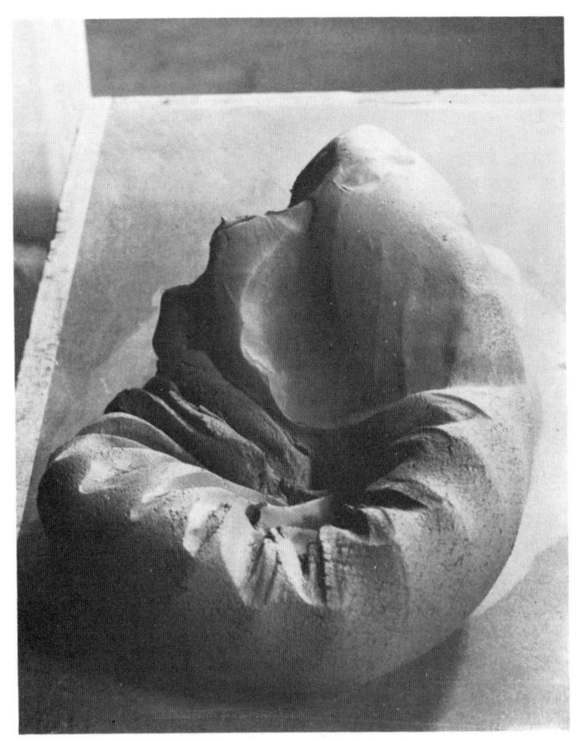

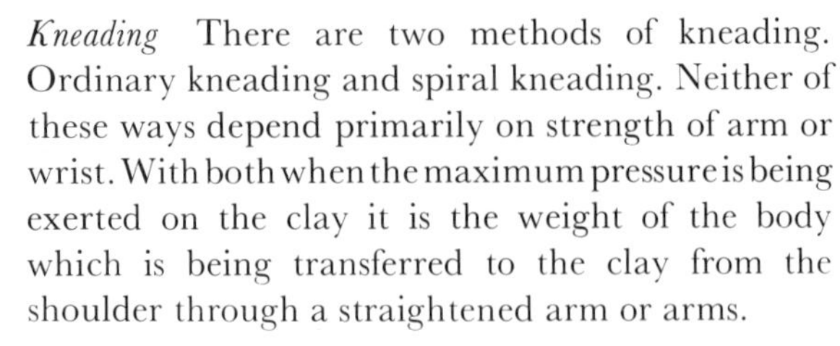

Kneading There are two methods of kneading. Ordinary kneading and spiral kneading. Neither of these ways depend primarily on strength of arm or wrist. With both when the maximum pressure is being exerted on the clay it is the weight of the body which is being transferred to the clay from the shoulder through a straightened arm or arms.

7 The effect of spiral kneading on clay is to press it out into a shell-like form. The movement is simple yet difficult to describe and is usually initially difficult to do. It is a knack which at one moment seems impossible and at the next can be done and it is difficult to say what has suddenly made it possible. The right arm is the one through which weight is exerted, the left hand merely contains the clay and turns it.

8 The right hand is at the top of the spiral above the concave centre.

9 As the clay is rolled forward and as the body leans forward pressure is exerted and the clay is folded downwards towards the centre.

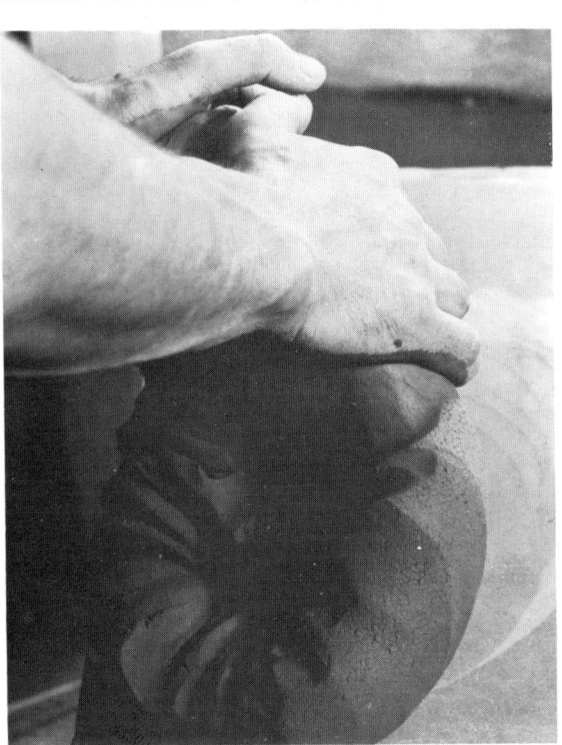

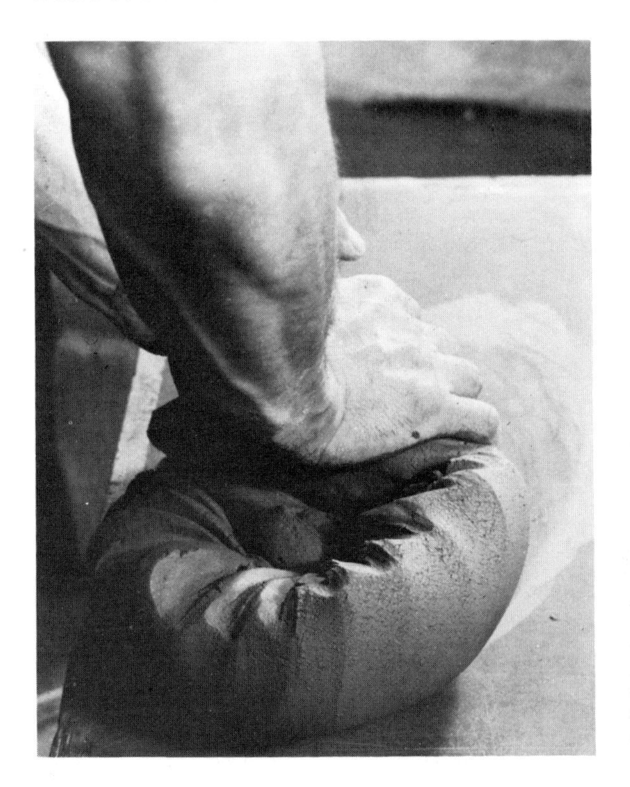

10 As the roll continues the left hand is lifting the clay back to the starting position and the right hand is moving forward to be above the clay for the beginning of the next roll.

11 At the end of the roll no pressure is being exerted on the clay the left hand is pivoting round slightly and the right hand is raised to be above the clay.

12 The hands have returned to the original position to begin the downward pressing motion again.

If the above movements are thought of as being right handed it should be said that it is perfectly possible to do spiral kneading left handed.

Quite large amounts of clay can be spirally kneaded. It should be an easy rhythmical motion, the correct height of the table is the all important factor in determining this. Tables or benches are unlikely to be too low and in schools if they are too high it is a good idea to have firm timber blocks of various heights for people to stand on.

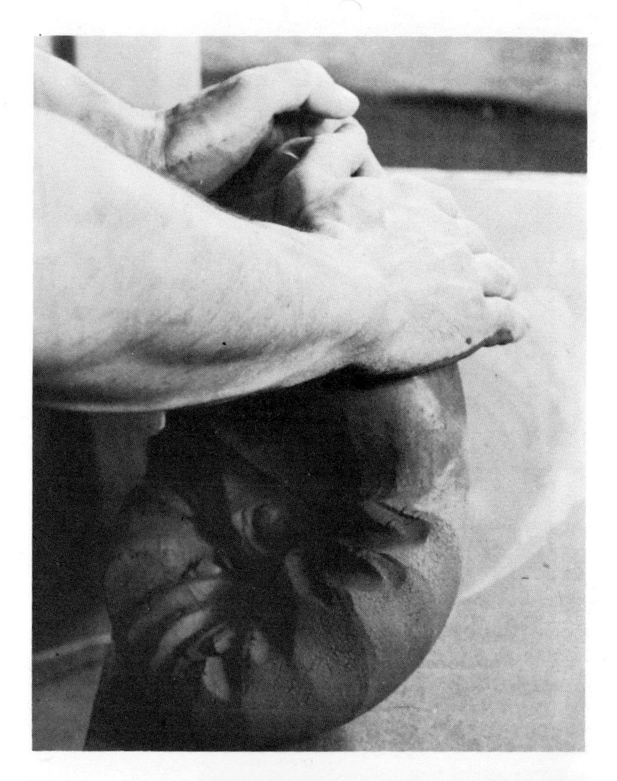

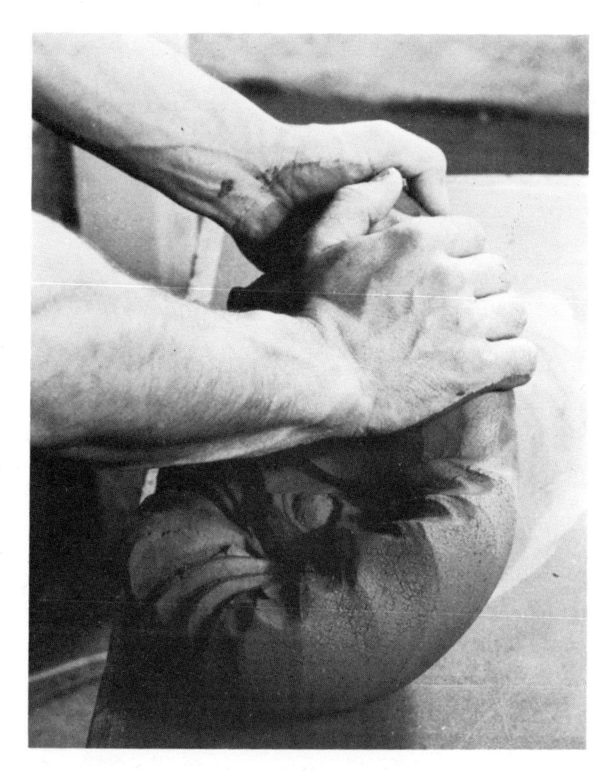

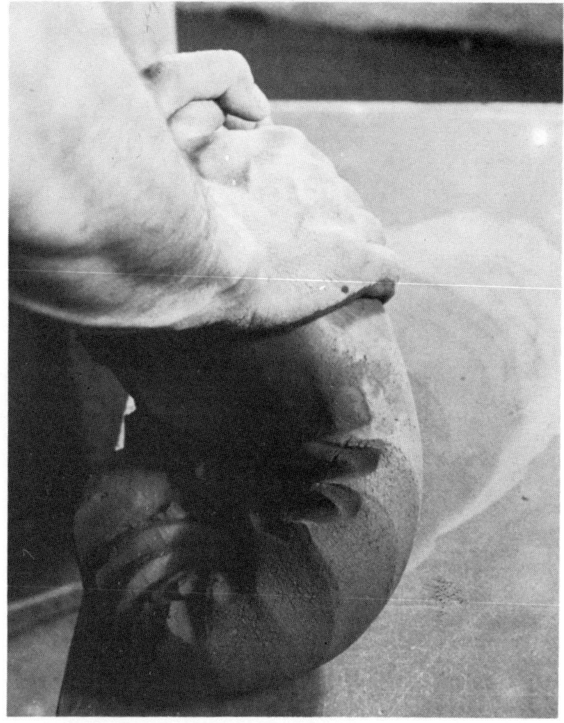

Ordinary kneading is usually learnt far more quickly than spiral kneading and being able to do it usually makes it far easier to pick up the knack of spiral kneading.

13 Both arms exert equal pressure on the clay and press it into a symmetric form.

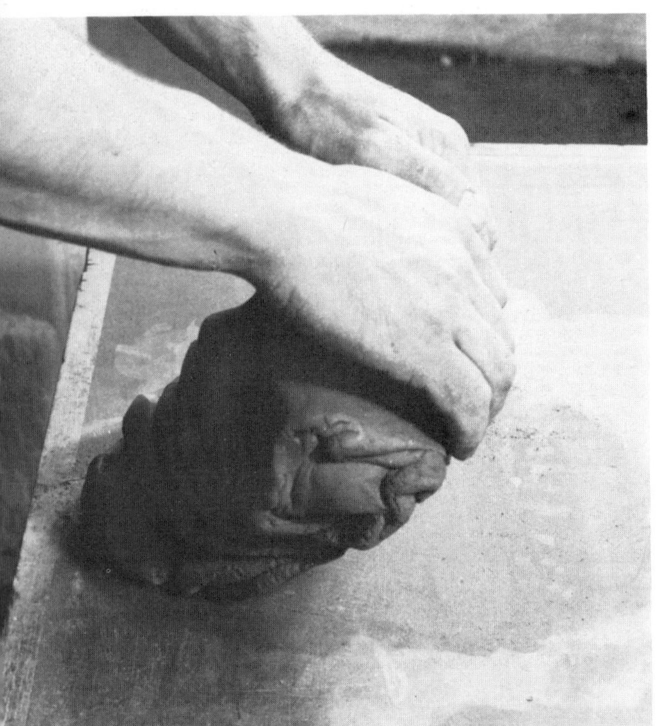

14 At the beginning of the movement the hands are well over the mass of clay.

15 The first part of the movement is downwards and backwards pressing the clay into a thicker roll.

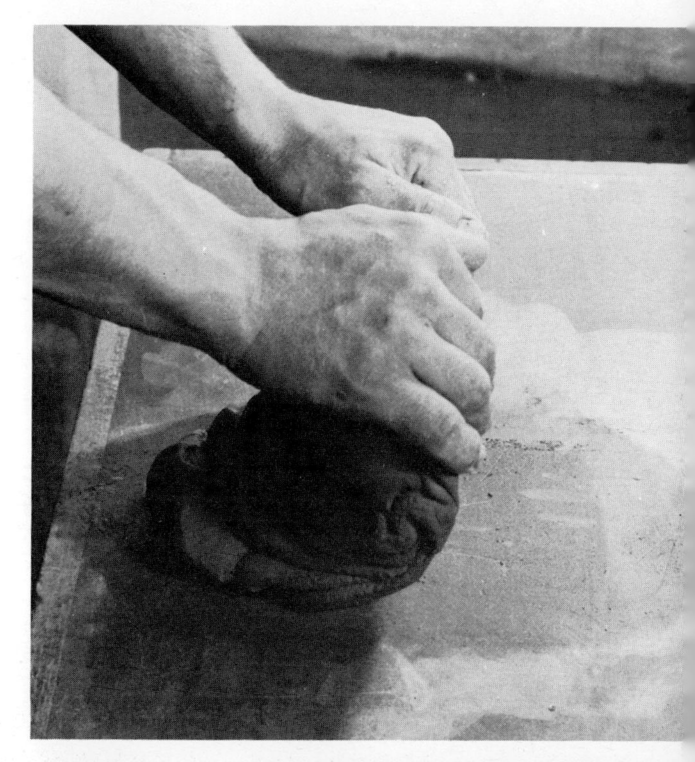

16 The hands then press forward strongly. At the end of this movement both hands 'walk' forward on the clay to raise it to a more vertical position and to be above it for the next movement. An additional part of this process is to turn the clay through 90° and begin fresh rolling movements occasionally.

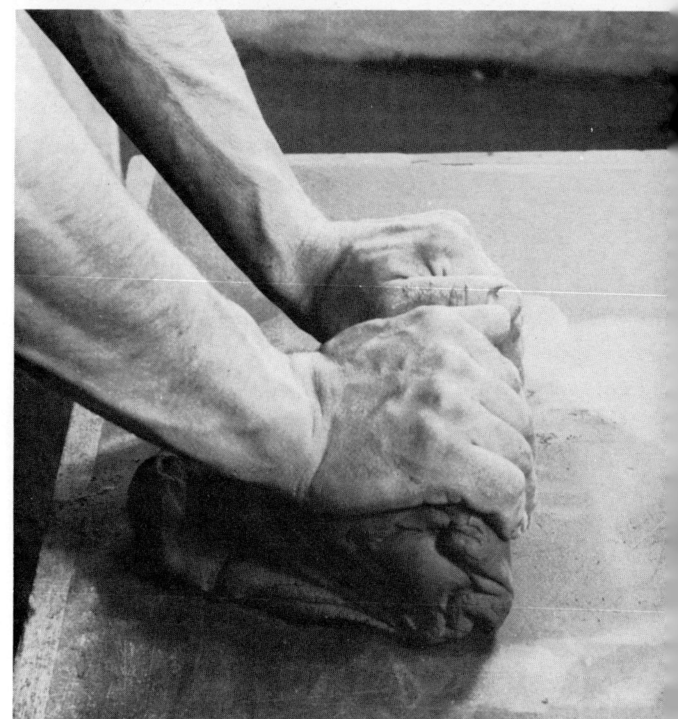

Section Two Clay forming processes

It would be wrong to see each of the descriptions of processes which follow as being the only possible variation of the method. The important things to learn from these descriptions are the principles underlying the processes. This should facilitate the most important learning process which is the acquisition of understanding which comes through first hand experience.

All of the processes described exploit one facet or another of the plasticity of clay. Plasticity is not however a single quality and clay itself is a remarkably variable material. Most clays can fairly easily be formed in several different ways but it is important to learn that some clays are more easily formed in some processes than others. A clay which is good for press moulding may be difficult to throw and a clay which throws well may be difficult to join in slab building. But these are only possibilities, certainty can only come with particular clays through first hand experience.

The ease with which a clay may be formed in a particular process is only one of several factors which need to be considered when clay for a particular piece of work is being chosen. Two of these factors are the firing temperature of a clay, and its fired colour. These three, and other factors such as texture, need to be considered together whenever clay is being selected for a particular piece of work.

It is worth pointing out that there are two qualities on which virtually all the processes described in the sections which follow depend. One is the 'joinability' of clay of similar consistency with or without some joining material, slip or water. This quality is used in slab building, coiling, two piece press moulding and the application of handles. The other is the plasticity of clay – the quality which enables it to be spread, extended, formed into new shapes without breaking. This quality is used in throwing, pinching, the rolling of sheets of clay and the rolling of coils. The first quality allows forms to be constructed by the addition of units. The second allows forms to be made by the manipulation of a mass of clay.

The form of all pottery by whatever process it is made comes first and once that is decided a fundamental, if not the fundamental, aspect of the finished object is fixed.

SOME ASPECTS OF FORM

Later on there is a very brief discussion of some aspects of decoration which may be relevant to criticism or self-criticism. That discussion lists and briefly describes aspects about which questions may be asked. The nature of three dimensional form is so different to that of graphic decoration – quite apart from any other differences, form in pottery can exist, though it always has colour, without graphic decoration whereas graphic decoration in pottery cannot exist without form – that is, it is easier to list types of form with which a beginner should experiment than to discuss different aspects which can be considered.

Initial work with form can investigate concavity and convexity, curvature and straightness, curvature and angularity, largeness and smallness, heaviness and lightness, complexity and simplicity, proportion, the relationship between inside and outside of hollow forms and the nature of edges between inside and outside form. Every form has a surface and that surface is marked inevitably by the processes of forming but the nature of the marks can be controlled during making or modified after making. Many forms rest on a flat base. The nature of the form as it meets this base qualifies to an extraordinary extent the visual nature of the form. All these factors are ones which can be considered as the basis for experiment by beginners and aspects for appraisal by all.

As with all techniques and materials the forming processes available in pottery all have particular potential qualities. Real freedom and understanding in the choice of means and of intention can only be achieved if there is at least a measure of first hand experience of the possibilities inherent in the different processes. Ideas can occur and be modified simply by experiment with processes. With the range of possibilities that exists the sensible basis for the rejection of particular processes is the understanding of first hand experience not the presumptions of ignorance.

PINCHING

17 A bronze age pinched bowl from Cyprus with a pierced pinched handle. About 2200 BC.

The simplest and most direct way of making a pottery shape is to hollow out a ball of clay by pinching it between the thumb and fingers. It is the method by which much of the pottery of the earliest cultures was made.

As a process pinching can lead to very varied results. Forms can be elaborate and asymmetric or they can be simple and symmetric. Historical examples of pinching invariably fall into the latter category of simple symmetric forms but this has much more to do with the intended function of these forms as cups and bowls, and to the context of pinching as a standardised production process, than to the nature of the process. Removed from the context of a production process pinching offers a very wide range of qualities.

It is instructive to experiment widely with the process, aiming on the one hand at a spontaneous and unpredictable freedom and on the other at a planned control. Initially it may seem easier to work very freely but some aspects of the process will only be grasped, and with them some important aspects of the nature of the plasticity of clay, if attempts at controlled simple forms are made until reasonably predictable results can be achieved.

Whatever is the intention with pinching and whatever the end result the nature of the process, the way the form is enlarged, is identical. The clay is pinched out and allowed to stiffen a little and then again pinched out and so on until the form reaches the chosen dimensions.

18 For initial attempts the ball of clay should be no larger than will comfortably sit in the palm of the hand. The clay should be soft but not sticky. The ball should be tapped to a reasonably round shape and should be free of surface folds which might cause cracks to develop in the edge at a later stage.

19 The thumb is pushed into the middle and pinching begun. If the right hand is used for pinching the action is pinch, turn a fraction, rest in the left hand, pinch, turn and so on and the clay is slowly revolved in the left hand.

20 It is best to start at the bottom and, in widening circles, to work towards the edge. The edge should not be over thinned too soon or it will tend to dry quicker than the rest and may be liable to crack as the softer clay below it is extended in later stages of pinching. Pinching should stop when the form begins to feel liable to sag seriously and it should be put on one side to stiffen a little. When an uninterrupted period of time can be given to pinching, several forms can be worked on during the same session.

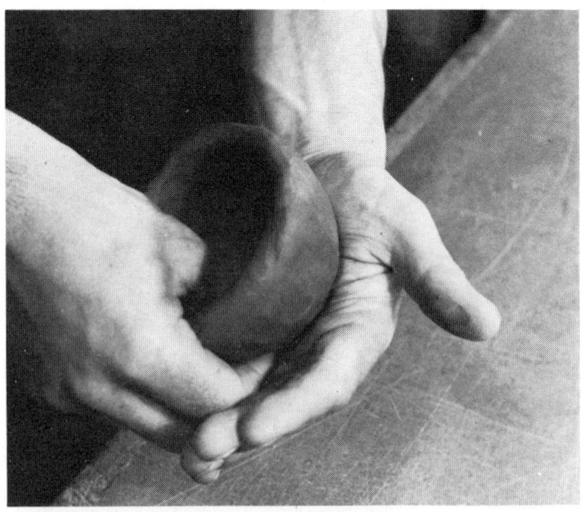

21 When the clay has become a little more rigid pinching can be resumed; again working from the bottom and keeping a reserve of clay in the top edge.

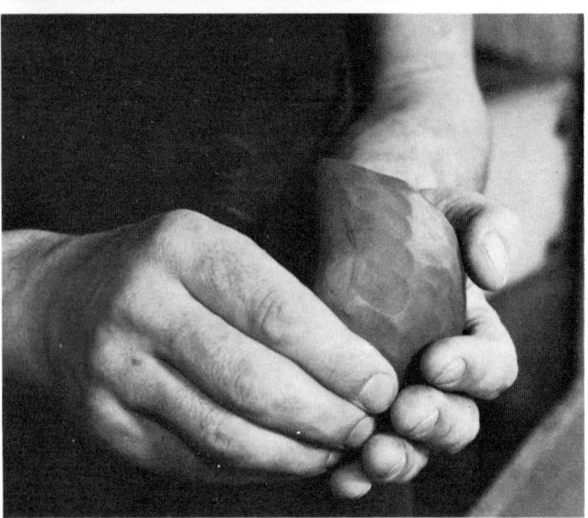

22 The secret of achieving an even wall and a symmetric form is obviously in maintaining an equal pressure in each pinching action and in maintaining an equal spacing between each pinching action.

23 After the form has been pinched several times with appropriate hardening intervals between it will have become progressively more rigid and texture of the pinching will have become closer and closer.

24 It is at this point when the main form is much firmer and is virtually self supporting with little or no tendency to sink when placed on a flat surface that the advantage of keeping the top edge thicker will be fully appreciated. Being softer it will be relatively more plastic than the form below and can be pinched in various forms to complete the whole form. Had the edge been thinned earlier this freedom would not have existed and attempts at the modification of over hardened edges invariably lead to cracking.

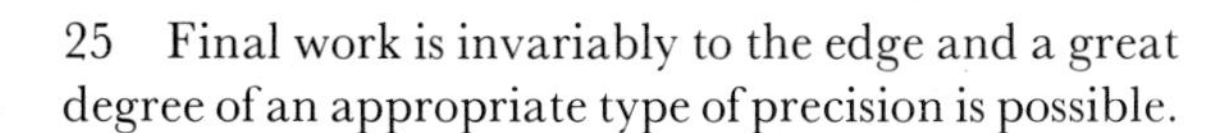

25 Final work is invariably to the edge and a great degree of an appropriate type of precision is possible.

It should be possible to complete pinched forms of either simple or complex nature without them drying too much and being liable to crack. If this seems to be a problem the clay can be dampened with a sponge and then left until the surface has lost its stickiness, or the fingers, rather than the clay directly, may be dampened with a sponge periodically while pinching is being done.

While it is entirely possible to finish pinched pots without resource to any tools it is of course equally possible to tap them gently to achieve a different quality of line of form and to impress, scratch and otherwise modify their surface.

Historically pinched pots were frequently painted with fine textured iron bearing slip or with haematite and burnished. This is a simple process and there does seem a certain appropriateness about the combination of a pinched surface which is modified by the not dissimilar progressive circular stroking action of burnishing.

To burnish clay with haematite the clay should be leather hard. The haematite is mixed with water to a creamy consistency and this is painted on to the clay. When it has lost its tackiness sufficiently to be gently rubbed without being rubbed off the clay the surface is burnished by rubbing with a small smooth pebble or the back of a spoon or any appropriately shaped smooth hard object. The high gloss which can be achieved is retained without much dulling after the firing but if subjected to temperatures much over 1000°C a great deal of the gloss may be lost. Haematite produces a warm terracotta colour when fired in an oxidising atmosphere and rich blacks if heavily reduced.

By describing burnishing in such close proximity to pinching there is a danger that some inevitable connection is implied. Though the qualities of the two processes may be not inappropriately combined it must be said that there is now no inevitable connection. The historical connection between the two processes is, however, entirely logical. Most burnished pinched pots preceded the discovery and use of glaze and before glaze burnishing was probably the best available method of making an earthenware pot less porous, less rough to the touch and easier to clean. Most burnished pinched pots were cups or bowls so the historical connection is an understandable one.

While the acquisition of a degree of methodical control has been stressed and for an understanding of the possibilities of the process it is important it should also be said that the thin, cracked, frayed edges which can also result from pinching are another important aspect of the possibilities.

COILING

While pinching exploits the plasticity of clay for the extension of a form, coiling exploits the plasticity of clay for the making of units with which a form can be built up. The process of coiling offers therefore a far greater range of possible scale. Coiled pots can vary from the minute to the monumental. Because the type of plasticity required is particular to the process, the type of clays which can be used is very varied. Clays which could not easily be rolled into sheets or would be difficult to pinch or throw may be excellent for coiling. Coarse non-plastic material may be added to coiling bodies which would be inappropriate for other forming techniques. But this is not to say that smooth and conventionally plastic clays are inappropriate.

26 The rolling of coils is a relatively simple process and yet it is surprising how many people have difficulties. Oval coils and hollow coils are frequent experiences with beginners. The lump of clay from which a coil is to be rolled should be squeezed into a roughly cylindrical shape. The first thing to do when rolling begins is to roll the ends to blunt points. If the end starts with a hole in it the rolling of the coil can produce a largely hollow coil. As soon as the ends are formed, and in time this becomes an automatic and very quick action – more of a check that there is not hollowness than a conscious sharpening – pressure can be applied and rolling begun.

27 Obviously to use two hands is quicker but until co-ordination and confidence are achieved beginners may find it easier to use only one. The problem of oval coils usually occurs at the point when the backward roll of the coil is changed to a forward roll. It is important throughout the process of rolling coils that the downward pressure which thins and extends the coils is reduced to nothing at the beginning and end of each backward and forward roll. If it is not, obviously, the momentarily stationary round coil is squashed oval. The downward pressure can be greatest at the middle of the forward and backward stroke. Sometimes beginners find it helpful to thin the coil only on the backward roll towards the body. Clay consistency for coiling is important. It should not be so soft that it tends to stick to the bench otherwise making the coils is obviously difficult and it should not be too firm otherwise the adhesion of coil to coil will be poor. The ideal condition varies from clay to clay. But the important consideration is not the ease of rolling but the quality of adhesion of coil to coil.

28 The hands move from side to side as they roll the clay backwards and forwards thus constantly affecting the entire length of the coil. The clay itself should never be dampened directly during rolling otherwise it simply cannot be rolled out. With certain clays and consistencies of clays the area of bench on which the coiling is done can be wiped with a damp sponge. This gives the coils a tacky surface which helps in achieving a good join. Unless they are for immediate use coils should not be simply left on the bench when rolled. In fact it is much wiser to roll a few often than to make a large number. If more than can be immediately used are rolled they should be laid on to polythene and wrapped up to prevent the surfaces becoming even slightly dried. Cracks in coiled pots due to this cause may only reveal themselves after a biscuit or even a glaze firing.

Before any coils are used a base is beaten or rolled out and, if necessary, cut to size. The use of a banding wheel or other turntable is essential if coiling is to be done easily and with control. Coiling a cylindrical shape is an instructive initial exercise.

29 The beginning of the coil is firmly stroked down on to the base and then the coil is laid gently in position.

30 It is possible to coil in a continuous spiral but initially it is wiser to build in rings – especially at the base of pots. If this is being done the coil is pinched through at the point of join and the end is firmly stroked down on to the other attached end of the coil. The banding wheel is now revolved slowly and the coil pushed down slightly as its position relative to the base is checked.

31 The inside surface of the coil is now stroked firmly downwards on to the base. The other hand supports the pressure of this action preventing the wall from being distorted.

32 The outer surface is now stroked downwards. The other hand supports the pressure of this action.

33 Coils do not need to be stroked together singly but they should be joined while it is still possible to support both sides of the wall and while the clay is still soft enough to join easily. The join produced in the coiling process should not only be the superficial one produced by the stroking together of the surface but should also go right through the wall as the soft clay of the coils is pushed together by the pressure used in stroking the surface – the effectiveness of this second join depends very importantly on the consistency of the clay.

34 It is by no means inevitable that coiled forms should have fingered texture. After joining has been done with the fingers it is possible to smooth the surface with a ruler or metal kidney or to otherwise alter the surface.

35 Whenever this sort of treatment is done to the surface of a form while it is being built it is important that a hand inside supports the external pressure.

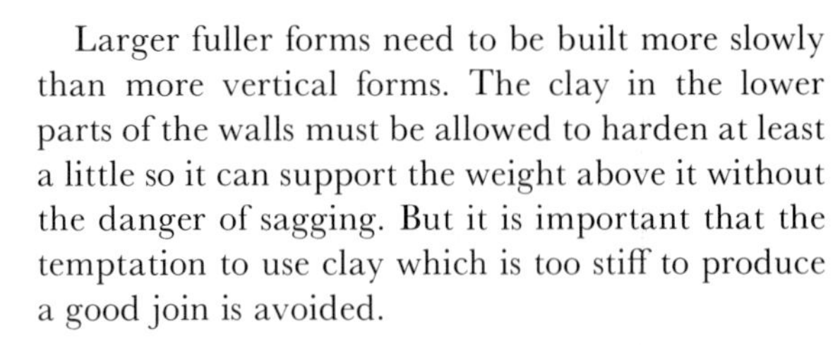

Larger fuller forms need to be built more slowly than more vertical forms. The clay in the lower parts of the walls must be allowed to harden at least a little so it can support the weight above it without the danger of sagging. But it is important that the temptation to use clay which is too stiff to produce a good join is avoided.

36 With practice, while one hand supports the loose coil the other hand places it in position on the wall. Simultaneously, while the thumb strokes down the inside surface the fingers support the outside, the inside join is made.

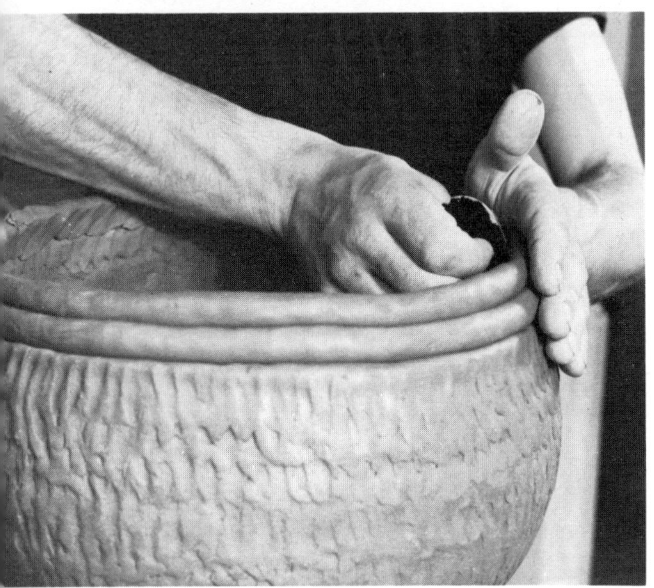

37 If the inside is to be smoothed with a metal kidney it is important that the outside of the wall is supported.

38 Unless the fingered texture is to be completely removed the extent of the initial vertical join marks, controlled partly by the number of coils joined up at once, will have a strong influence on the final texture.

39 The crispness of quickly fingered joins can seem to have become too sharp when clay is dry and fired and not infrequently the crispness is softened somewhat.

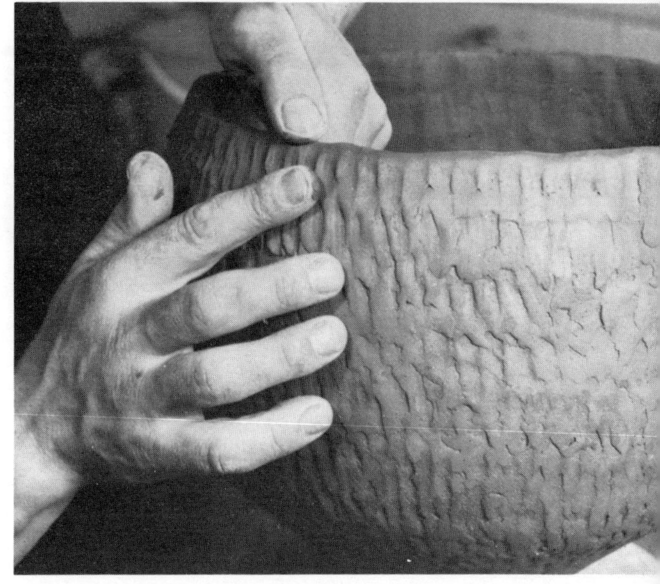

The textural possibilities of coiled surfaces are very wide. Marks can be left fresh or be modified. The marks themselves can create directions – herringbone, vertical, diagonal – and they can vary in scale. The surface can be lightly tapped with a wooden tool to give it a taut precise top surface beneath which the richness and variety of the fingered texture still exists.

A sensible initial aim is to be able to build fairly simple forms with confidence and control. A badly coiled wall is liable to sag and may collapse or crack. Once confidence and control have been achieved more elaborate forms can be tackled but coiling no less than many others is a process where freedom is arrived at through control.

SLAB BUILDING

Rolled out slabs of clay of almost any consistency can be used for building forms. The process can be treated as a free, plastic way of building or it can be treated in a non-plastic way and, obviously, there are possibilities between the extremes.

In its freest use soft clay can be bent into forms, with or without support. The only technical process here is the joining of the surfaces which meet. These can often simply be pinched together when this is possible and not visually undesirable. If slabs are to be joined without the visual changes effected by pinching together the surfaces which meet should be painted with slip and pressed together. Very varied free surfaces and forms can be made by building with soft slabs but it should not be forgotten that, if the form is to be certain to survive, joins that are made need to be well enough made to stand the drying and firing stages every clay form has to go through.

At the other end of the scale rolled out slabs can be allowed to dry to a firm leather hardness and then be precisely measured and cut and used to build angular forms.

Everyone at some stage and from a position of experience has to draw a dividing line for themselves about forms and qualities that are right in pottery, pottery being the somewhat fragile thing that it is when finished. Both the free plastic and the precise non plastic aspects of slab building have the inherent problem that forms may be made which pose the question: 'Is this right as pottery?' Even if the answer is always 'Yes' it is important that the question is asked. Slab building is not, obviously, alone in posing this question but it does probably pose it more quickly than other processes.

The most usual stage for joining slabs together is at a medium soft leather hard stage. A valuable aspect of initial exercises in slab building is that the joining processes used can be applied in other contexts as well as slab building.

40 The rolled out slabs are carefully cut or trimmed on the sides that are to be joined just before they are joined. Cuts should be truly vertical (where the joins are at right angles, obviously) so that the surfaces to be joined meet well. The surfaces which meet are scored. There are two variations: the two slabs on the left are scored with a wooden tool, the two on the right with a sharp metal tool.

41 The more broadly scored marks made with the wooden tool are thoroughly but not too liberally smeared with slip and the two surfaces are brought together. The initial movement in joining can be to slide them from side to side until they begin to grip, then the entire joint should be worked along firmly pushing the two pieces together.

42 The slip that is squeezed out of the join is removed.

43 The more finely scored marks have water squeezed onto them from a sponge and the marks are re-scored and water is again applied. This process which can be repeated two or three times works up a slip out of the slab itself and generally softens the surfaces which are being joined. When the surfaces are sticky with slip they can be brought together and treated in the same way as if slip had been applied as in the first variation.

44 When the two sides are assembled they too are prepared for joining and the two are brought together.

45 At this stage great care should be taken to methodically work on each of the two new joins. These, obviously, will always be less accessible than the first two.

46 Whenever slab built constructions are made it is easiest to work with the greatest dimensions flat for as long as possible so that a tall form becomes so at the latest possible stage. Long joins are much easier to make with the clay flat on a bench.

Once joined together a slab built form can be either worked on straight away or allowed to harden up considerably before it is finished.

Generally speaking the open top of a slab built form (if it is to be open) is only made to its intended form and detail once the form is completed. The edges which form the base should be precisely cut before any joining begins so that the assembled form can be placed onto a slab (as in illustration 46) but to attempt to cut the top edge as well is not worthwhile. Slab forms usually depend largely on the relationships between the dimensions of their various parts so to leave the top to be detailed and the height to be determined at the end is, as well as being easier, a more sensible alternative than trying to complete the form while it is still flat and in pieces.

MODELLING

The term 'modelling' is not a specific one. It can mean the making of models for moulds for use in casting or pressing. It can mean the building up of solid forms in clay for casting in another material or, when hollowed, for firing as terracottas. Loosely the term is often applied to the making of non functional pottery.

In fact, of course, all the techniques in this section can be applied in the making of pots or the making of sculpture. Whatever the dividing line may be between pots and sculpture it is certainly not defined by technique.

This brief section aims to describe one process that is conventionally used in non functional contexts and is not covered elsewhere in this book.

There is a limit to the thickness of clay which can be fired. Bricks, of course, are thick and are fired. But bricks are usually made out of open, often sandy, clays which dry readily and which, being open in texture, fire fairly easily. Problems arise, however, with smoother, finer clays and it is certainly possible to say that the closer the texture of the clay the more difficult is the firing with objects that are thick. Objects that are built up solid if they are of any scale and have to be fired are hollowed out at some stage prior to firing.

The history of pottery abounds with examples of superb objects which are functionless. The forms of many of these can often be seen to have been made by coiling, slab building, pinching, or one or another of a variety of moulding or casting processes. These forms can be added to by building directly onto them with clay. This in one sense is modelling. Providing the modelled additions are well joined onto the main form there are no real technical problems attached to the process. Illustration 48 is an example of this.

47 Salt glazed English miniature figure about 1755 *Victoria and Albert Museum*

48 Figure from a ridge tile of a tomb, Chinese Ming Dynasty *Victoria and Albert Museum*

Modelling on any large scale when one of the traditional processes of hollow building has not been used requires different treatment. Any form built up of solid clay which exceeds a thickness of about 50 mm has to be cut in half, hollowed out and rejoined. There is no particular difficulty attached to this but it is important that it is done at the right time. The clay must be hard enough to support its own weight when the form has been hollowed. The clay must not be so hard as to make rejoining risky. The clay must be soft enough to allow the possibility of subsequent building onto the surface. The right time for most such work is a softish leather-hard stage. It is a complete mistake to finish a form which has to be hollowed too much before it has been cut and rejoined because the joining may tend to distort the form slightly and will certainly disturb the surface considerably.

Forms being treated in this way should be built up of clay of even consistency, should be basically shaped and proportioned and then be allowed to harden the right amount. They are then simply cut into two (or more pieces) along the longest dimensions with a wire and are hollowed out to an appropriate thickness with a wire modelling tool. The halves are then joined together in whichever is the preferred method. Then they can be worked to a finished state in form, detail and surface.

Complex forms may need support at all stages of the making process. The best way of providing this support is with clay of the same type as the model. This can shrink, dry and be fired with the model and thereby offer support both during making while the clay is plastic and during firing. It is a good idea to build complex or potentially fragile forms on a kiln shelf so that the risk of breakage when the form is dry and has to be lifted into a kiln is minimised.

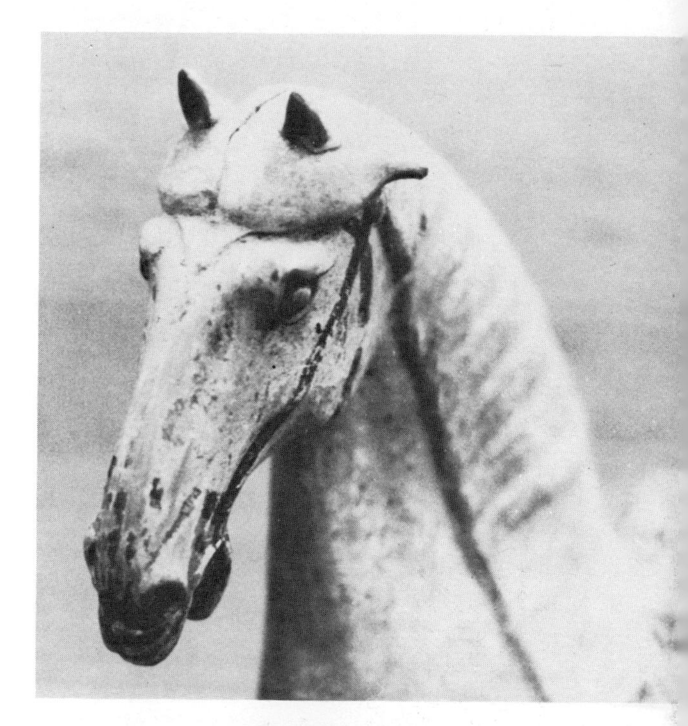

49 Chinese, Tang Dynasty *Victoria and Albert Museum*

50 Indian terracotta *British Museum*

MOULDED POTTERY

Moulding in one or other of its many manifestations was used in early times by most cultures. These earliest moulds were made of fired clay and were intended for use with plastic clay. At later times moulds of wood, alabaster and metal were used as well but today the commonest material for mould making is plaster. Plaster was known at an early date – it was used by the Egyptians, the Greeks and the Romans for wall surfaces and for making casts – but only fired clay not plaster moulds are known. Exactly when it was first used for pottery moulds is not known but Piccolpasso in his *The Three Books of the Potter's Art* written between 1556 and 1559 mentions the use of plaster moulds in Italy. The use of plaster for pottery moulds in England is said to date from about 1750 when it was introduced from France by Ralph Daniels.

Plaster of paris is burnt gypsum, so called because it was found in considerable quantity in the raw state at Montmartre. In England it occurs extensively in Derbyshire. Gypsum is calcium sulphate, $CaSO_4 2H_2O$; it is also known as alabaster and, when colourless and translucent, as selenite. This gypsum is ground to a powder and heated to about 120°C, when it boils and gives up an equivalent of water and becomes a hemihydrate $(CaSO_4)_2\ H_2O$, and very unstable, having a great affinity for water. Plaster of paris should always be stored in a dry place. When added to water it forms a creamy fluid mixture which sets in from five to fifteen minutes (depending on its type) and dries in from twenty four to seventy two hours or longer (depending on conditions) to a hard, porous solid. The process is not reversible. Once mixed and used the plaster cannot be reconstituted.

There are many types of plaster. The several types which can be of use in pottery vary in fineness, speed of setting and ultimate hardness. Types are made which are specifically suitable for moulds for slip casting and, an especially hard one, for 'block' moulds needed for the mass production of moulds. All plaster can deteriorate if stored in damp conditions which can cause it to set without ever developing a serviceable hardness or even not to set at all. It is wiser to buy plaster in 25 or 50 kilogram bags than the very much smaller amounts sometimes available from chemists which may have been stored for a long time and may never develop the hardness necessary in pottery moulds. Once the plaster bag is opened it is safer and less messy to empty the plaster into a plastic or galvanised dustbin which has a well fitting lid.

Mixing of plaster

Plaster is always added to water. Mixing can be done in a bucket or bowl. Mixed plaster may occasionally be poured from a jug but it is far easier to mix properly in a wide-topped container. Judging the amount of water and the resultant amount of mixed plaster which is needed for a specific job is largely a matter of slight experience and common sense.

51 Any container should not be much more than half full of water before mixing begins. The plaster is sprinkled through the fingers and from the palm over the entire surface of the water.

52 Two hands may be used but the action is always one of sifting never one of dropping in large amounts suddenly which would tend to form trapped pockets of unwetted plaster which would tend to form lumps in the mix.

53 Plaster is added until it begins to build up above the surface of the water. At this stage plaster is still added but only to those parts of the bowl where the plaster level is still below the water surface. No more plaster should be added when there are no areas of clear water left and when there are some areas where a thin layer of plaster is above the water surface. The bowl is then left for a minute or two, no more, while the water penetrates through the plaster on the surface.

54 Mixing is done by spreading the fingers wide and moving them from side to side on the bottom of the bowl. This should be vigorous enough to set up a motion or several motions within the mix, sucking plaster from the top towards the bottom and forcing it from the bottom to the top. The action is slower than, but not dissimilar to, that necessary to create frothy soap suds in water to which detergent has been added. The action should not break the surface otherwise air bubbles will be sucked into the mix rather than expelled from it. When it is being effective where the plaster rises to the surface a steady stream of popping air bubbles will be seen.

55 With a good mix if the hand is raised steadily from the plaster it will be covered with a creamy opaque coating of plaster. If the hand colour can be seen then the mixture is a little on the thin side.

The plaster is now ready for use. Plaster should never be mixed until everything else is ready for its use. From the moment that it has been mixed organisation and efficiency are essential. In less than fifteen minutes the soft creamy mixture becomes a hard solid. Fifteen minutes can see the creation of a considerable mess but there is no need for this to be the case. All bowls and tools and one's hands should be cleaned before plaster sets onto them.

One piece press moulding

The process of using plastic clay in one piece moulds is most frequently manifest in the making of dish forms. Jigger and jolley and decoration by sprigging are also related to the process. See pages 79 and 150.

It is generally agreed that it is easier to model convex or positive forms rather than to carve concave or negative forms. Certainly this is true of simple forms. (Some complex forms, perhaps for sprigging, are more easily carved into plaster.)

56 It is not necessary to work on a squared board nor is it necessary to build up the form out of smallish lumps of clay but if this approach helps as it well may with symetric forms then it can be used. This approach does allow for a rather more thoughtful controlled gradual modification of a form than the usual alternative which is to take a lump and beat and carve it into shape.

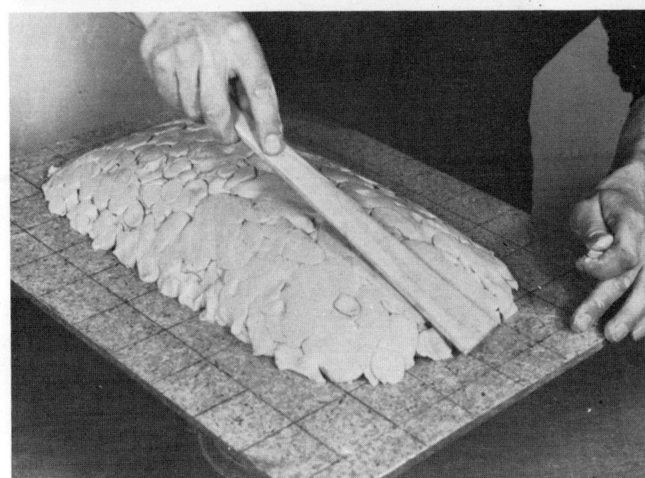

57 Whatever method is used to build up the basic form it is far simpler to finish the form if the final layer is built up with smooth clay of an even consistency. Profiles can be easily established and adjusted by tapping the clay with a shaped batten or a large modelling tool. Small holes and hollows can be ignored at this stage.

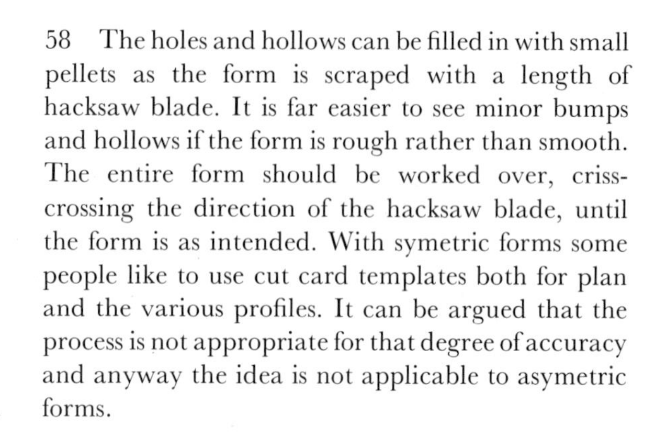

58 The holes and hollows can be filled in with small pellets as the form is scraped with a length of hacksaw blade. It is far easier to see minor bumps and hollows if the form is rough rather than smooth. The entire form should be worked over, criss-crossing the direction of the hacksaw blade, until the form is as intended. With symetric forms some people like to use cut card templates both for plan and the various profiles. It can be argued that the process is not appropriate for that degree of accuracy and anyway the idea is not applicable to asymetric forms.

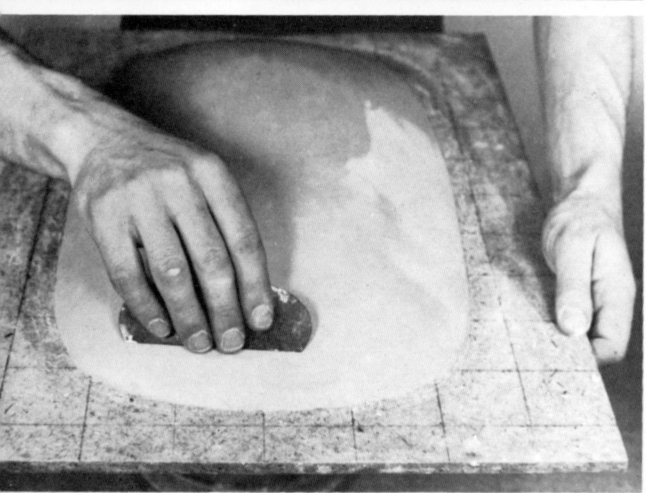

59 Before casting the last stage is to smooth the hacksaw texture off the clay form. This is done with a steel kidney and if the clay is of even consistency should be an extremely quick operation. Scratches in the clay surface will come out as raised lines in the cast and for this reason it is arguably quicker and better to leave any persistent such marks and minor indentations in the edge to be cleaned up at the plaster stage. More roughness or serious bumpiness may result if the attempt is made to fill these.

There are two different ways of casting a dish mould. One produces a mould of even cross section and requires slightly more skill and experience in the use of plaster. The other produces a mould of uneven section but is easy and quick to do.

60 To make a mould of even cross section a coil is placed around the model at an even distance of about 38 mm from its edge. It should be firmly thumbed down to the board on its outside only, then the board should be soft soaped.

Immediately the plaster is mixed it should be poured in handfuls so the entire clay form and the board up to the coil are covered in plaster. The quicker this can be done the smaller is the chance of any air bubbles being trapped on the surface. The table or board can be gently raised and dropped to remove any bubbles that may exist.

61

62

63 The plaster is then left for a minute or two until it stops being creamy and runny and becomes cheesey and thicker. Then working very quickly an even layer of plaster is methodically built up over the whole of the first layer of plaster by methodically working round the form.

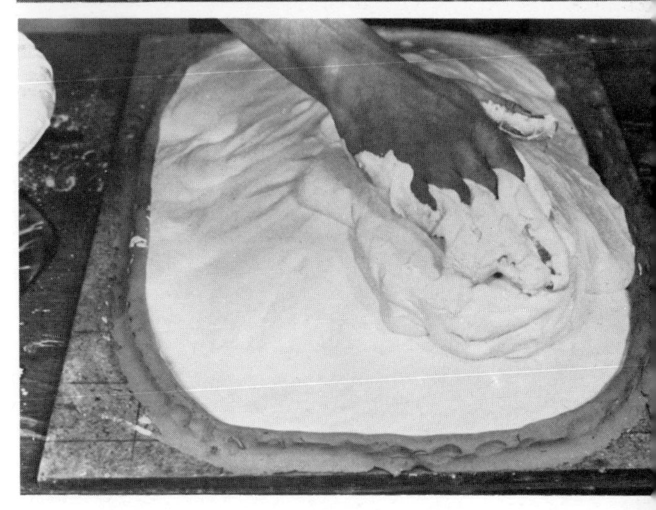

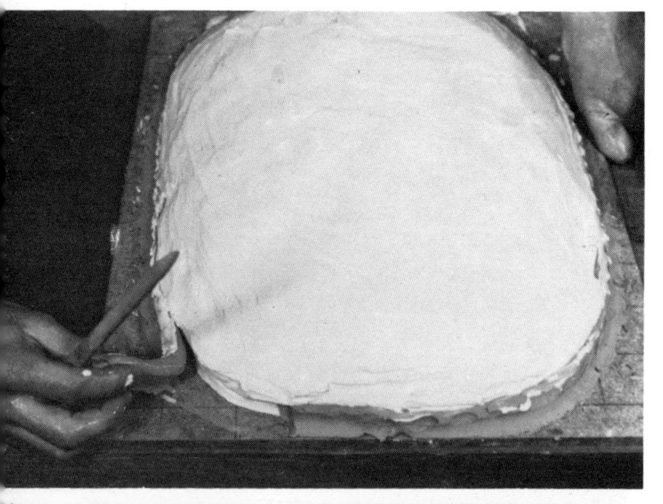

64 This is smoothed as it is added. A bucket of water should be at hand to wash the hands in and to wet the plaster if need be as smoothing is done. As soon as the plaster has been built up the coil, the real function of which was simply to retain the runny plaster, is removed.

65 Plaster can be washed off the coil in the bucket of water.

66 Then the edge can be tidied up. Great care must be taken not to go too far into the flat edge of the mould.

67 After ten minutes, or longer depending on the type of plaster, the workboard is placed over the edge of the table and is gently leant on. This should release it and the whole mould and model can be turned over. Sometimes the clay of the model is securely stuck and there is nothing much else to do except to bend and push until something moves. Sometimes running water into the crack between plaster and board helps to separate the clay from the mould so it can be removed leaving the clay stuck to the board. It is better if possible to see that the clay does not stick to the board.

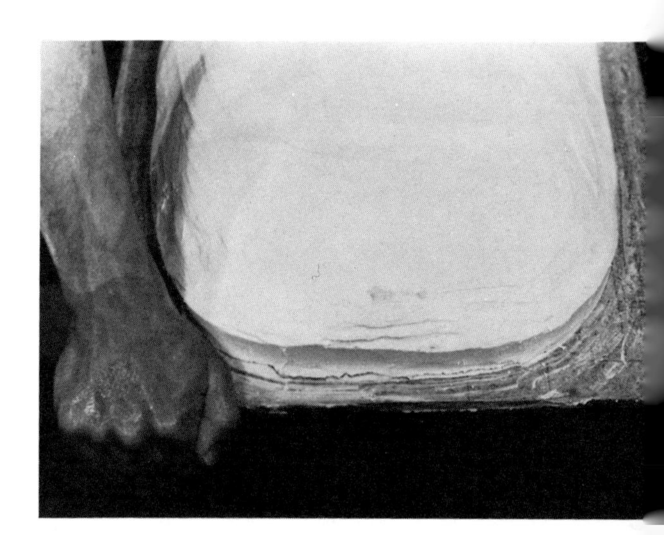

68 When model and mould have come away from the board together the clay can be removed by pushing firmly down fairly near the edge which should push some clay outwards.

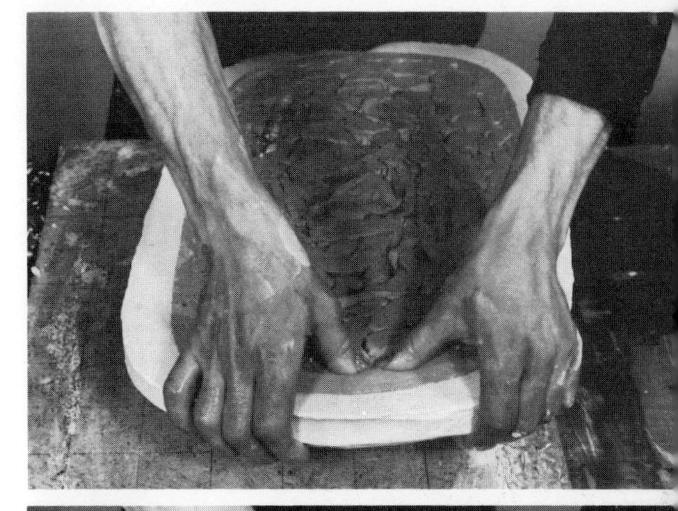

69

70

If this raised clay is then lifted the entire model can usually be peeled out whole.

The alternative method has the disadvantage that on a large scale it produces extremely heavy moulds.

71 A piece of lino or vinyl is taped to the correct dimension and placed over the form.

72 It is positioned at an even distance from the clay model edge and held in position by a coil.

73 Plaster is poured in until the model is well covered.

74 The lino is removed as soon as the plaster sets and the sharp cast edge should be cut back.

75 The edge of a mushroom mould is bevelled back to the beginning of the convexity at whatever is the preferred angle. It is a good idea to keep a mushroom mould permanently in its hollow mould to prevent its vulnerable edges becoming chipped.

The pressing of shapes can be done directly into both the types of mould described. When this is done the smooth worked-on surface of the original clay lump forms the underneath surface of the dish. If a 'mushroom' mould is cast from a hollow mould then the smooth, worked-on surface becomes the seen inside surface of the pressed forms. It is not right or wrong to work on a mushroom mould or in a hollow mould but it must be appreciated that the results are different – the edge form especially is inevitably different.

To make a mushroom mould the hollow mould is first sized to prevent plaster sticking to plaster. There are various kinds of size used in plaster casting – beeswax and pure turpentine; shellac and methylated spirits; olive oil – all of which have their uses but for pottery moulds the best size is a solution of soft soap and water. A piece of soft soap the size of an egg is added to a cupfull of water and is stirred over a gentle heat until it is dissolved. The solution will be thick, almost syrupy. The solution can be used immediately and will keep indefinitely if bottled.

When using soft soap sizing, if the plaster is dry it should first be dampened. A little soft soap is poured into the mould and rubbed round with a fine sponge which will produce a lather. After a minute or two the lather should be wiped off with water and the process repeated twice more when surface of the mould will be shiny. Water splashed on to the surface will sit on it in droplets. The non-absorbent surface will effectively prevent the plaster sticking. The important thing about soft soap is that unlike the other sizing mixtures it does not permanently affect the porosity of the mould.

When well sized the hollow mould is set up, on clay if necessary, absolutely level and plaster is poured in until it just overflows the hollow mould and spreads a small distance on to the flat edge. The plaster is now left to become cheesey when a previously prepared collar of vinyl or lino is laid on to the middle of the new plaster and is filled up with plaster to produce a stem on which the mushroom mould can stand.

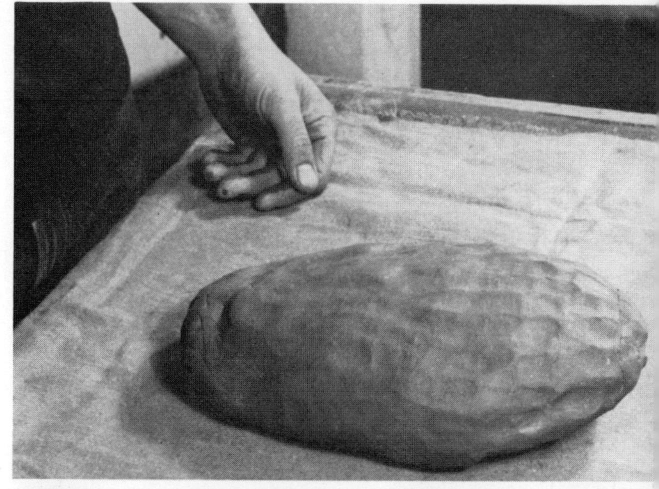

Rolling out clay is a very simple process but it is surprising what a labour it can become if a few simple points are not followed.

76 Even before it is placed on the rolling out cloth the prepared lump of clay can be flattened.

77 With large pieces a great deal of effort can be saved if before it is ever rolled it is further pushed and beaten out by hand.

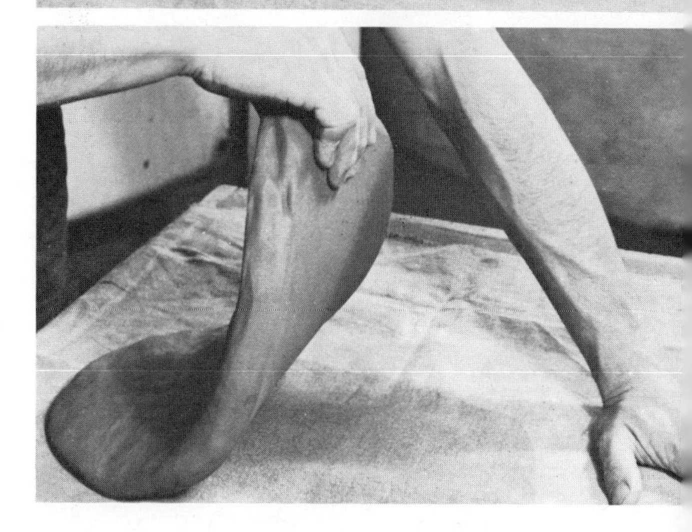

78 The important point to remember both when beating out the clay and subsequently when rolling it out is that when pressure has been applied to the whole surface the clay is stuck to the cloth. Being stuck it cannot freely move when pressure is applied to it by rolling. Therefore each time the complete surface has been rolled or beaten the clay must be freed from the cloth.

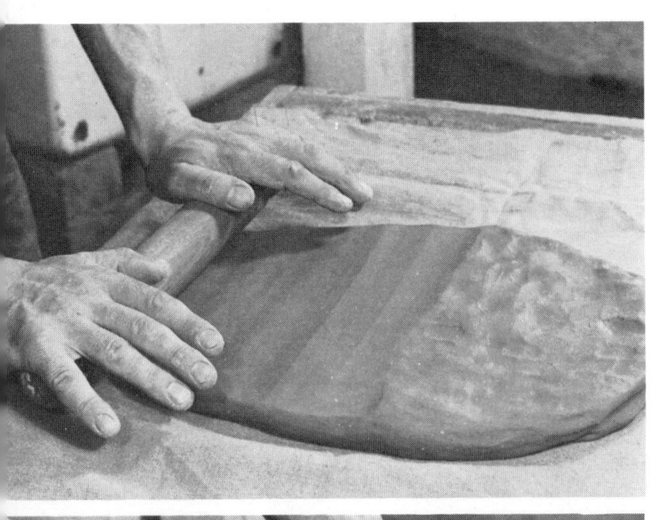

Here the clay is first rolled from the middle towards the body then from the middle away. Then it must be freed.

Two or three actions like this will fairly effortlessly thin out large sheets of clay.

79
80

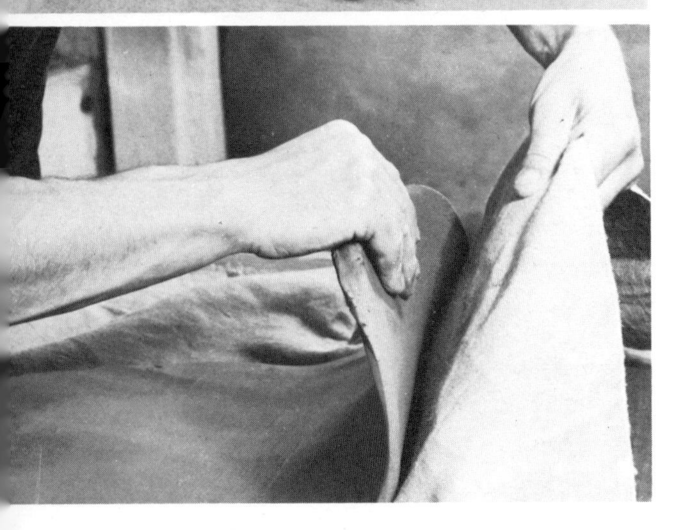

81 Once the clay becomes thin, if the sheet is large, it is safer to lift clay and cloth and to ease the cloth away like this rather than to attempt to lift the clay directly off the cloth.

When the clay is the required thinness it should not be freed from the cloth and quite strong pressure can be applied to roll out any unevennesses.

82 Rolled surfaces are sometimes slightly open in texture and a final action can be to smooth the surface with a metal or rubber kidney.

To press a shape over a mushroom mould the mould should start off on the table but a banding wheel should be handy.

83 The clay firmly stuck to the cloth is lifted with cloth folded over its corners – this eliminates any danger of the clay falling off the cloth.

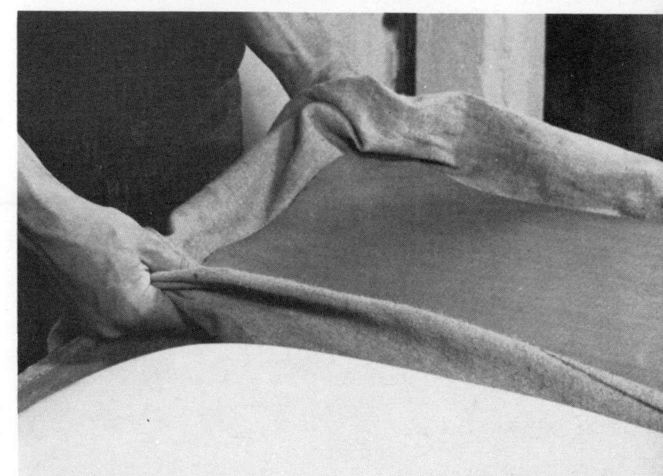

84 The clay is laid on to the mould. With shallow shapes it is possible to press the clay on to the mould while the cloth is in place, with deeper shapes the cloth needs to be removed for the clay to take up the form.

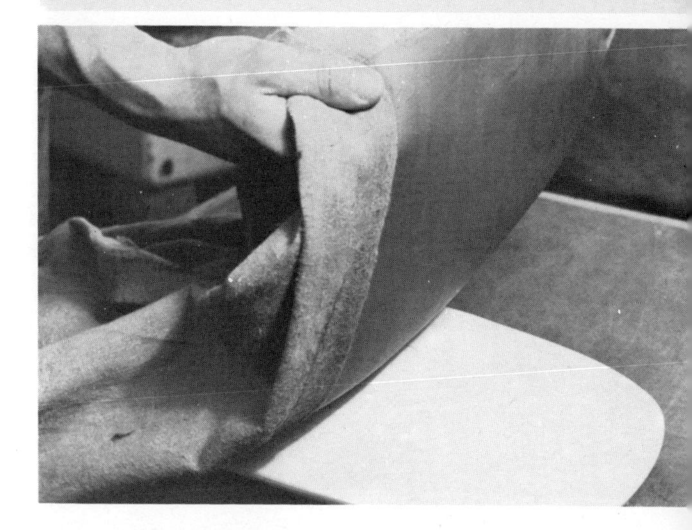

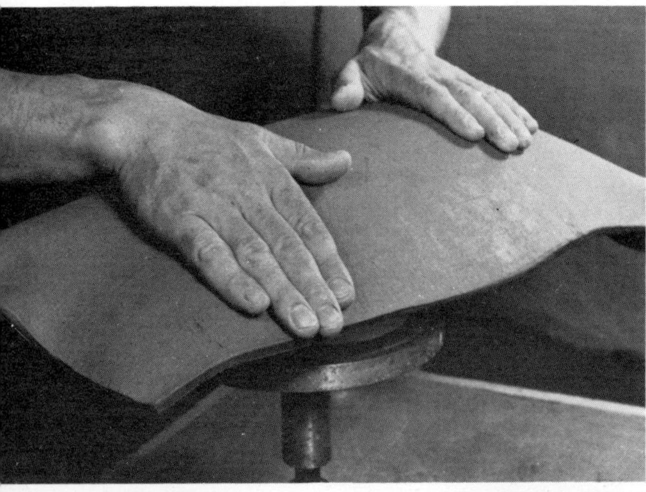

85 With the cloth removed the clay sheet is gently pressed over the mould.

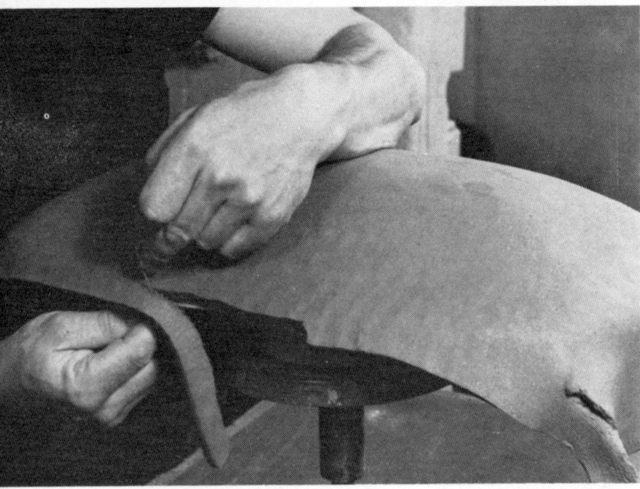

86 This pressing will reveal the edges and the larger amounts of excess clay can be trimmed off.

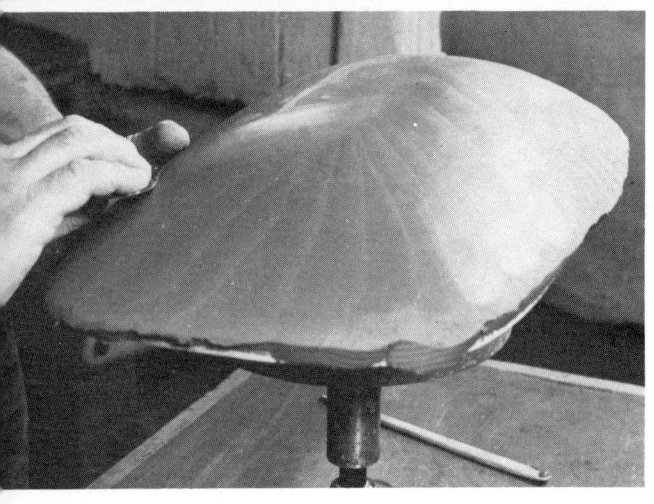

87 The clay is then deliberately and firmly pressed on to the mould starting at the middle and working outwards and finally going round the edge.

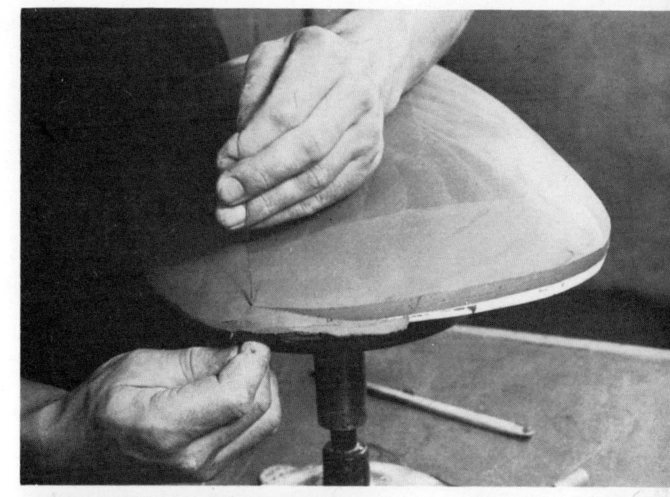

88 The edge is then finally trimmed. The bevelled edge of the mould and the angle at which the wire is held above the form determine the angle of cut.

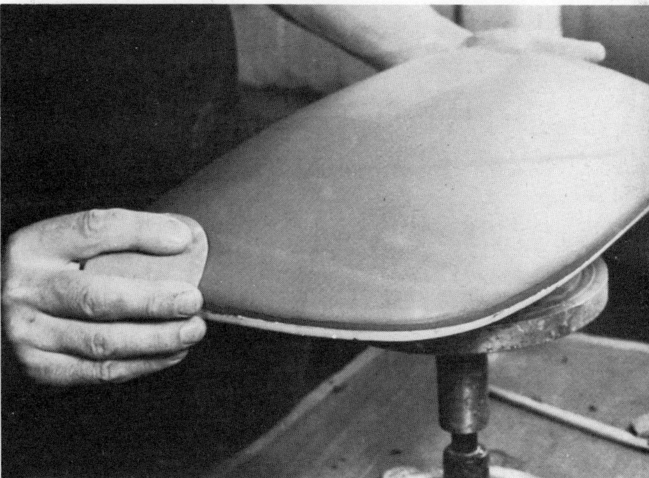

89 Finally the entire form is smoothed with a rubber kidney again working from the middle outwards and finishing by going round the edge.

Shallow dishes can harden on their mould but where production of a number is envisaged or when a form is deep it is more convenient and, in the latter case, safer if more moulds are made to receive the finished dishes once they are firm enough to be removed from the mould. These additional moulds are made by casting from the back of a dish as shown in figure 89, a flat edge level with the dish edge first being built up with clay. The whole process is rather involved if only a few dishes are to be made but when large production is planned it is standard except where the dishes have large flat bases and can dry on a table or shelf without warping.

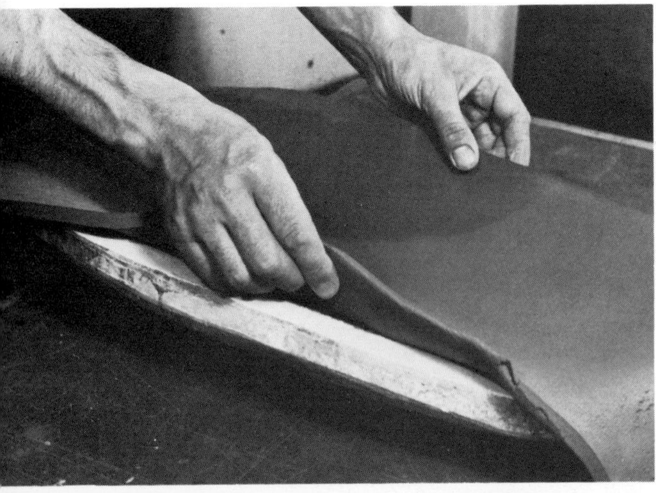

Making a dish in a hollow mould is straightforward.

90 The clay is laid on the mould smooth side down and as soon as the cloth is removed it is eased down into the mould.

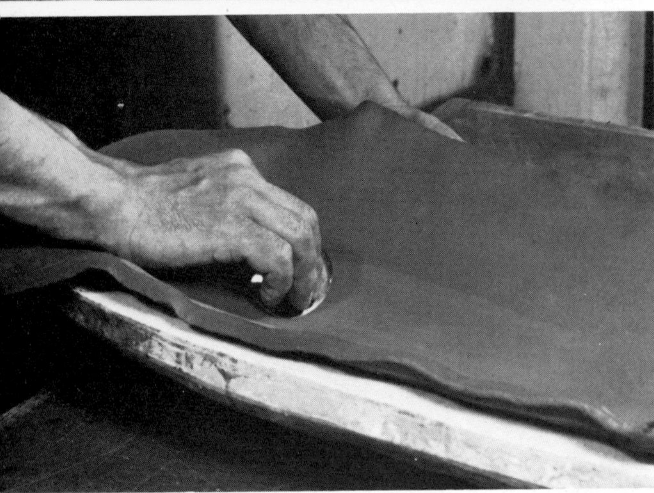

91 The clay is pressed against the mould with a metal kidney working from the middle outwards.

92 The excess clay is then removed.

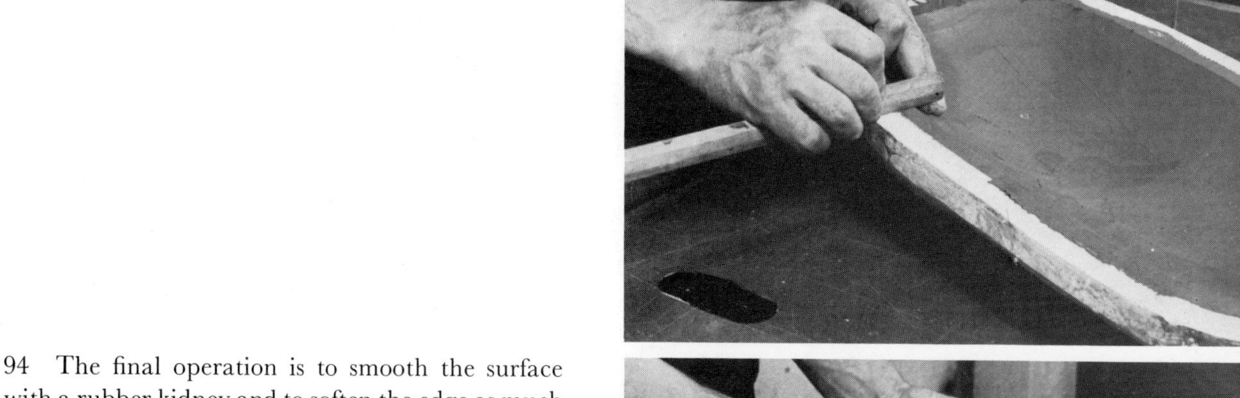

93 The edge is then cut level with the mould edge using a wooden tool or an old wooden ruler and doing only a little at a time.

94 The final operation is to smooth the surface with a rubber kidney and to soften the edge as much as is thought necessary.

With both hollow and mushroom moulds the edge of dishes need some attention at the leather hard stage when the dish can be removed from the mould.

Obviously the process of press moulding open forms is extremely flexible. Clay can of course be added on to newly made dishes. Whether a dish is made in a hollow or on a mushroom mould is determined either by the kind of edge wanted or, very importantly, by any techniques of decoration which are being used, some of which may require the use of either one or other type of mould.

Two piece press mould

The process of press moulding plastic clay in two piece moulds can be used on different scales to produce either hollow or solid casts. The process was very extensively used in Roman times for the production of figurines and oil lamps. In the eighteenth century it was used for making teapots and other vessels, spouts, handles and, with metal moulds, for clay pipes.

95 The mould is bedded into clay to the halfway mark and a flat ledge is built out. On this flat ledge a small strip of clay of roughly triangular cross section is placed so that its inner edge meets the point where the flat clay ledge touches the model. Vinyl or lino is then fixed around the clay bed and plaster is poured in to well cover the model.

96 As soon as the plaster sets the clay bed is removed and the first half of the plaster mould is then prepared by cutting not less than two deep 'V' shaped grooves into the edge and thoroughly soft soaping the top surfaces and 'V' grooves. If the original clay strip stayed in the plaster it can be left, if not the groove is filled up with clay and a second triangular shaped strip is added exactly over the first. Vinyl or lino are then fixed and the second half of the mould is cast.

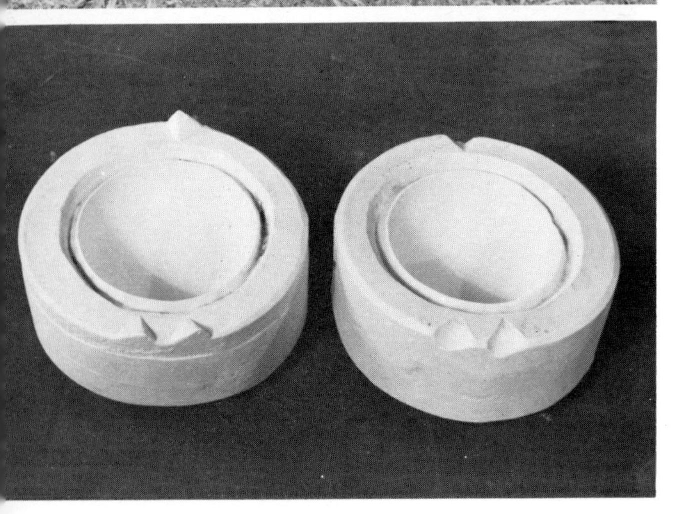

97 The mould is separated as soon as the plaster sets the model and the clay in the grooves are removed and all sharp edges on the outside edges of the mould are bevelled.

The exact method adopted for putting clay into press moulds depends very much on the scale of the moulds and the nature of the surface of the model and is largely a matter of common sense. With small moulds intended for solid casting clay is simply methodically pressed into the mould and one side is very slightly overfilled. A larger mould for hollow casting with a complex surface requires different treatment and is perhaps the only process which is not obvious. A ball of clay is pressed into the deepest part of the mould and the clay is then pressed outwards from this area. New clay is added to the upper surface of the original piece and is spread outwards so no join shows. Clay is never added to clay on the surface of the mould – this leaves a very clearly visible join.

98 With most smallish moulds a pinched hollow piece of clay is dropped into the mould.

99 This is then methodically pressed against the mould surface working from the middle outwards.

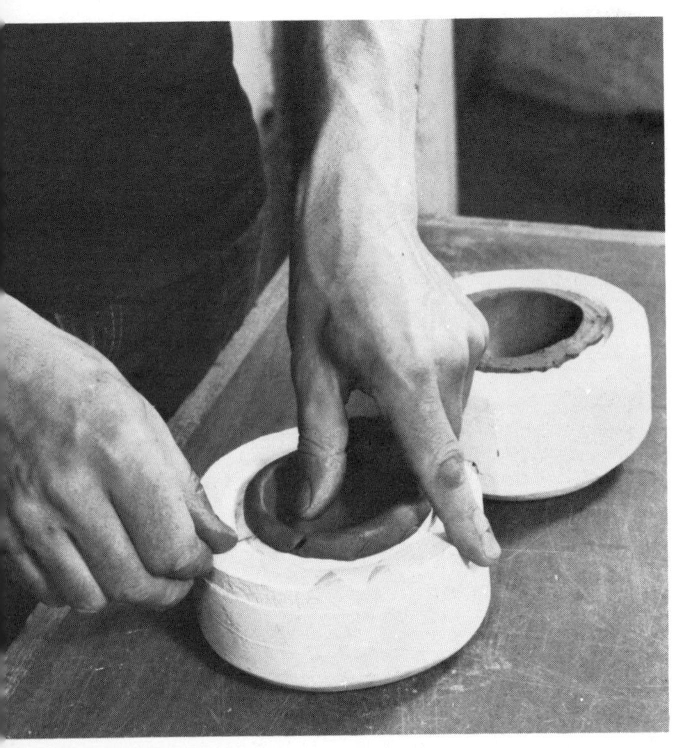

100 The edge is then either trimmed flush and subsequently pushed up a little or, as in this case, trimmed slightly high.

The edges of the clay are then slipped or sponged with water, as preferred, and the two halves of the mould are brought together using the 'V' grooves to locate them. The two halves of the mould are then pressed firmly together until the plaster of the two halves meets all the way round. During the pressing excess clay will have been forced into the grooves around the form.

101

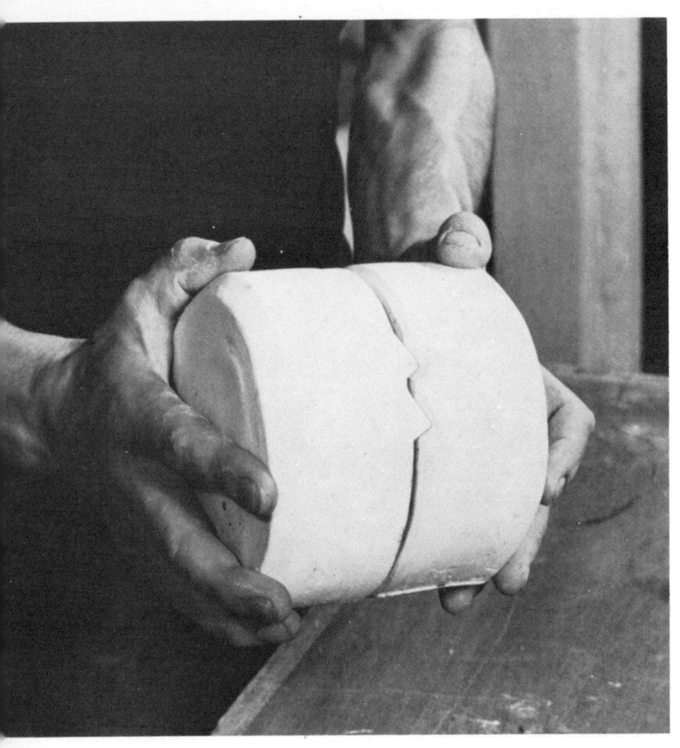

102

For the process to be successful the plaster edges which meet must be kept completely free of clay so that the true dimensions of the model are retained and the inside edges of the 'V' groove must not meet so well that clay cannot squeeze between them.

The photographs of this process show a completely enclosed form being made. When the form is an open one, like for example the agate teapots press moulded in the eighteenth century, the mould should have an open end so that the inside of the join can be worked on and smoothed while the form is still in its mould.

103

104

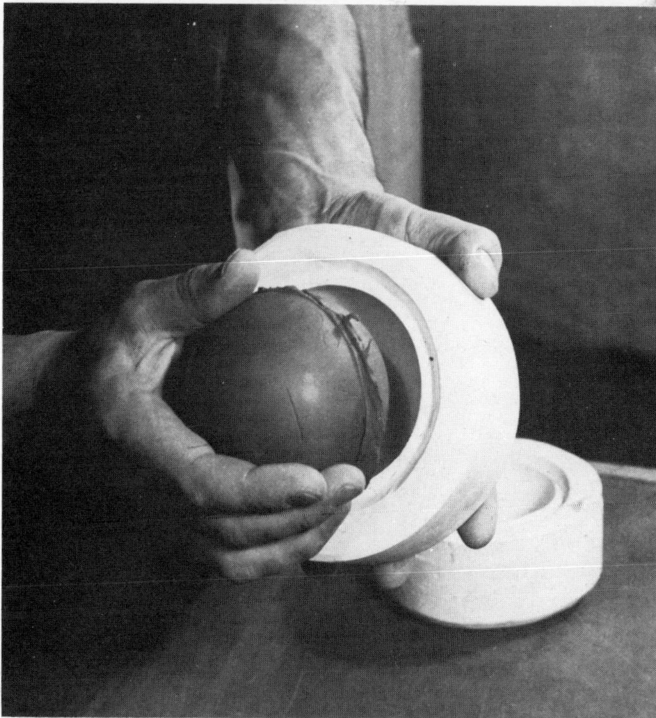

Slip casting

Probably the simplest way for a beginner to understand the nature of the slip casting process is for a simple one piece mould to be made. This can be turned from a clay lump on a wheel the one proviso being that the form is turned leaving a flaring step at its base which gives the mould an inward sloping edge to act as a reservoir for slip.

The mould is filled with slip well up the inward sloping edge. If the slip level sinks appreciably it should be topped up.

After ten minutes, or longer depending on the slip, the mould is emptied.

105

106

107

108 The mould is left to drain resting on sticks of uneven height. It is important that the sticks are of uneven height so that slip from the bottom can move down the sides rather than form droplets eventually standing up from the bottom.

109 As soon as the slip surface is touch dry, the slip on to the sloping edge can be trimmed off the cast.

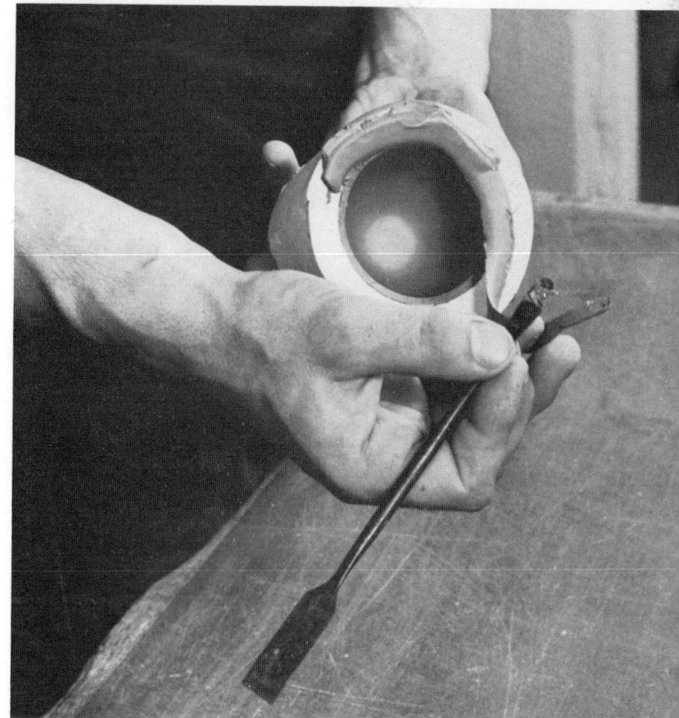

When the cast itself has shrunk clear of the mould all the way round the edge the entire cast will soon be free and can be removed.

While making a one piece drop-out mould may serve to demonstrate the behaviour of slip, one fundamental problem of mould making and slip casting is avoided and that is the problem of making good seams in the moulds. Seams are rarely, if ever, invisible on slip cast pottery but every effort should be made to make them so or they tend to be larger than expected.

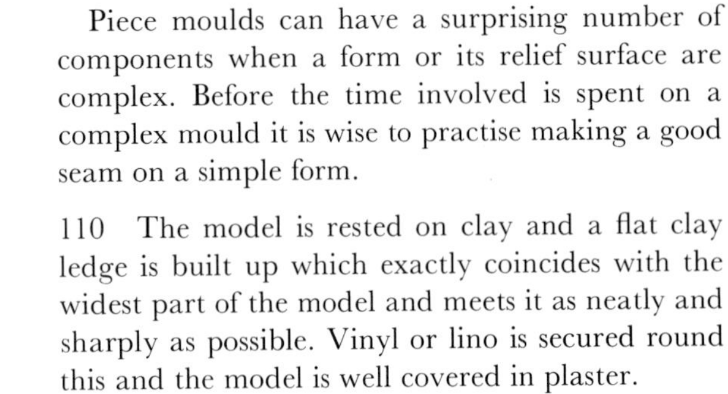

Piece moulds can have a surprising number of components when a form or its relief surface are complex. Before the time involved is spent on a complex mould it is wise to practise making a good seam on a simple form.

110 The model is rested on clay and a flat clay ledge is built up which exactly coincides with the widest part of the model and meets it as neatly and sharply as possible. Vinyl or lino is secured round this and the model is well covered in plaster.

111 The vinyl and clay are removed leaving the model sitting in plaster. Shallow locating indentations are made in the flat edge of the mould join and the top plaster surface is thoroughly sized with a soft soap solution. When vinyl has again been secured round the model and a small neat clay cone has been attached to the top of the model to function as a pouring hole, the top half of the mould can be cast.

112 As soon as the plaster has set the vinyl is removed, the mould is scratched so it always goes together the same way without error which could easily chip an edge. The mould is then separated and the model and clay removed, the mould edges bevelled and the whole mould washed and sponged clean.

113 The mould is then assembled and put away to dry. The mould should be thoroughly dried before it is used.

114 In use the pieces of a mould are either held together with cord tightened with small wedges or by cut sections of car inner tube. Whenever a mould is filled with slip the pouring action should be steady, not rushed and there should be no interruption of flow which will leave a line round the cast. If one container is insufficient to fill a mould a second full one should be to hand so that filling is uninterrupted.

115 Moulds should be filled right to the top.

116 Narrow topped moulds may need frequent topping up. Care should be taken always to keep the slip level above the highest point of the cast form itself.

117 Emptying narrow topped moulds may be tricky. Slip should never be allowed to glug out as this means air pressure inside the cast is being reduced which can pull the cast away from the mould. Air must always be allowed to enter as the slip is poured out. With narrow topped moulds this makes emptying rather slow, especially the initial stages when tipping backwards and forwards may be necessary, but even wide topped moulds should not be emptied quickly because the suction of a volume of slip can also pull a cast away from a mould.

118 The mould is left upside down to drain.

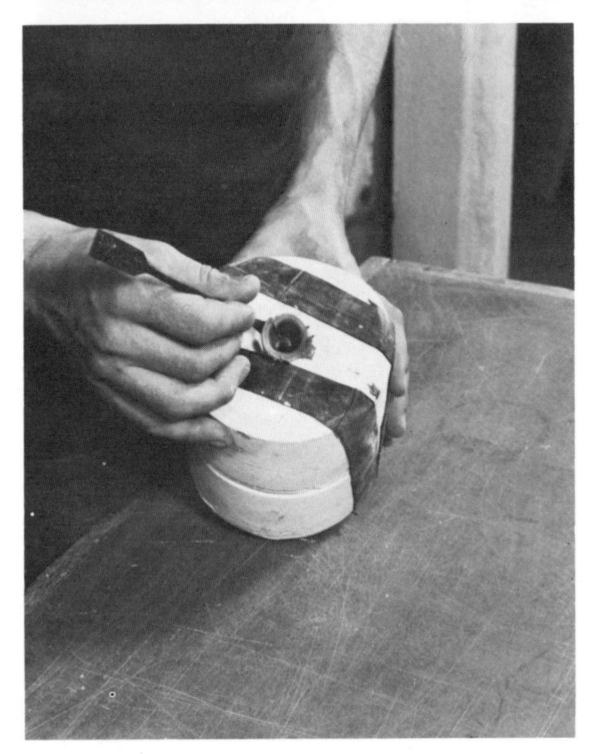

119 When touch dry the slip in the reservoir is cut away.

120 About half an hour later, longer usually, less only occasionally, this being dependent on the slip being used, the top half of the mould can be removed.

121 After a further period of time the cast can be completely removed when only a fine, neat line should show at the mould seam. This can be removed later with a small scraper or a damp sponge or chamois leather. This final tidying up and treatment of seam marks is called *fettling*. Good seams can be made almost invisible, bad seams however well they are fettled always reappear at the biscuit stage.

Slip casting is a technique full of possibilities but more perhaps than most it is worth really understanding the principle behind piece moulds and getting practice in the making of really precise seams. Good seams are far easier to make against a hard model than against clay so the advantages of easy mould making have to be weighed against the disadvantages of easy model making. As with everything else it all really depends on the particular work in hand and the qualities important in the finished work.

The making of casting slips Casting slips contain for every 100 parts by weight of clay and other ceramic ingredients about 35 parts of water and very small but vital amounts of deflocculents (usually less than 1 part each of sodium silicate and soda ash). The slip is made far more fluid by the deflocculents than it would otherwise be. An ordinary slip of comparable fluidity would contain 50 or 60 parts of water to every 100 parts of clay. This difference is vital to the process of slip casting. It means that the moulds become less wet during casting which means both that they can be used more frequently and that they do not deteriorate as quickly. It means that the drying shrinkage (and associated warping) is considerably reduced.

Casting slips can have very much less plastic clay than bodies used for other forming methods. If there is an excess of plastic clay it will take a long time for casts to form in the mould. If there is too little plastic clay casts will be very fragile in the dry state.

Casting slips can be made up both from plastic bodies or from powder. If no mechanical form of mixing is available it is easier to make them from powder. The first thing is to weigh out the water. The amount of water will be quite small if plastic clay is being used. Next the sodium silicate and soda ash are weighed out and are dissolved in some of the water – preferably hot water. This solution is then added to the rest of the water. (Sodium silicate is commonly available in two different viscosities, 75° and 150° Twaddell: It is very important that the specified grade is used.) When the water containing the dissolved deflocculents is ready, in the case of plastic clay, it is put into the blunger and the sliced or shredded clay is added gradually and in the case of powdered ingredients if a blunger is not available the ingredients are simply sprinkled on to the water and allowed to settle into it – this settling can take some time. When all the ingredients are wetted the mixture can be stirred. The final process whether the slip has been mixed mechanically or by hand is to pass it through a sieve to remove lumps.

Casting slip which has not been used for a day or two should always be thoroughly stirred before use. A portable hand blunger is ideal for this.

Probably because of its extensive use in the industrial context slip casting is too often thought of in terms of white firing bodies. In fact dark firing as well as light firing bodies, grogged as well as fine bodies and bodies through the whole range of firing temperatures can be made into casting slips.

The proportions of sodium silicate and soda ash needed to make a good casting slip vary. More plastic clays tend to need more soda ash and less plastic clays tend to need more sodium silicate. Sodium silicate gives fluidity to slip and tends to produce hard casts. Soda ash gives good draining quality but tends to produce softer casts liable to sag in the mould. In every case a balance of the two deflocculents is essential.

Jigger and jolley

Industrially, jigger and jolleying is pressing out clay shapes between a revolving plaster mould and a metal profile which is brought down onto or into the mould to form the side not made by the mould. The machine is very similar to a wheel and most wheels can be adapted to work as jigger and jolley machines.

Instead of a wheel head jigger and jolley machines have hollow cup-chucks or cup-heads into which the centred back of moulds fit so that the top is on centre. The arm to which the templates are bolted is counterbalanced so it can be swung up out of the way when not in use and is bolted to the frame of the machine. Deepish shapes like cups are made in hollow moulds which form the outside of the shape, the inside being shaped with a template. Shallow shapes, like plates, are made over convex moulds which form the inside of the shape, the outside being shaped by a template. Before shapes are made the template has to be accurately adjusted in relation to the stop on the arm so that it makes shapes of the correct cross section.

With shallow shapes a flat 'batted out' sheet of clay is thrown down onto the mould and is lightly sponged from the middle outwards before the template is brought down. Templates are lubricated with water while they are in use. With deeper shapes made in hollow moulds a ball of clay is dropped into the bottom and is sometimes thrown up the sides of the mould before the template is used. Jigger and jolleying is being done increasingly automatically.

Though considerable technical advances have taken place recently the idea of jigger and jolley is very old.

122 In about the third century BC a type of cup appeared the outside of which was clearly formed in a mould and the inside of which shows throwing marks.

123

124

123 The Romans refined this idea considerably. Moulds at this time were of fired clay and were simply rather thick bowls the insides of which were finely stamped before firing. These moulds, after firing, were simply fixed to a wheel head and bowls were thrown inside them. Frequently, as in this example, the bowl was thrown above the edge of the mould which allowed edges to be inward sloping which would obviously not have been possible in a mould. Separately thrown and turned feet were also frequently added to the bases of these bowls.

124 A fragment of a terracotta bowl mould from the workshop of M. Perennius 25 BC to 25 AD.

The Chinese also used moulds secured to a wheel but most often to form the inside of plates and shallow bowls. The process was always used to produce forms with fine linear relief designs.

125 An incised terracotta mould of the Sung dynasty.

These and other examples of the forerunners of the jigger and jolley process show an inventive use of the decorative relief possibilities of the process and a developed understanding of the degree of relief and depth of line which would release from a mould as the clay shrank.

Tiles

Tiles can be rolled out from plastic clay and cut. They can be hand pressed into wooden or plaster moulds. They can be wire cut from a block of clay using notched sticks. They can be slip cast. But the majority of tiles now made industrially are pressed from dust.

The very great advantage of pressing tiles (and other objects) from clay dust is that, because of the very low water content of the dust, shrinkage and warping (and drying time) are kept to an absolute minimum and a high degree of accuracy is maintained. The water content of the dust for tile pressing is low but is just sufficient to allow the considerable pressure of a tile press to bond the clay together.

Tiles, however they are made, offer exciting decorative possibilities in a unique way in pottery. The scale of an area of tiles can be far greater than is possible with any one clay object. Because tiles are basically flat and can be fired flat the use of glaze can be far freer than on three dimensional forms.

When tiles are being made it should be remembered that because no great degree of plasticity is necessary non plastic materials can be added to the body to control shrinkage and warping and to facilitate drying.

It should also be remembered that mass produced tiles are identical in size very largely for manufacturing convenience. The individual, for whom the making of tiles of identical size may be difficult, might make a virtue of making up an area with tiles of different sizes, some of which might be quite large – there are tiles from the town of Isnik in Turkey built into the walls of some pavilions in Topkapi Palace in Istanbul which measure over 122 cm × 46 cm.

THROWING

A high standard of throwing can be acquired only through experience over a period of time. In the initial stages of learning having a very clear idea of the simple principles behind the technique can greatly ease the learning process. Much of the highly developed technique of throwing is to do with understanding the qualities and limits of different clays and consistencies of clays as they are relevant to throwing. The descriptions which follow aim to show the basic movements. Whether learning is done through reading books, through watching demonstrations or through being personally instructed it is important to realise that the point to understand from these is not so much the precise position of hands or the particular fingers used but what the hands are doing to the clay. There is no one way to throw. However much individuals' methods may appear to differ what is happening to the clay is always the same.

Before throwing begins the first step is to centre the clay.

126 Many lumps of clay should be prepared so throwing does not have to be interrupted for clay preparation. The lumps should be beaten into neat balls and each new ball should be slapped down firmly on the wheel as centrally as possible.

127 The wheel is set in fairly fast motion, the clay and the hands are wetted and the arms rest on the sides of the wheel trough. Small pieces of clay with experience are centred virtually instantly. As soon as the clay is spinning smoothly without eccentric movement it is centred and the next stage of throwing can proceed but until and unless the clay is centred it is useless to proceed. The important thing to understand is that an inward pressure displaces the clay to a taller form and a downward pressure displaces it to a flatter form. These two pressures together centre it. The application of great force is unnecessary. Steadiness is far more important.

128 Though it is not strictly centring an action which often accompanies centering is to squeeze the clay up into a tall form and down again. This action mixes the clay internally in a quite complex way and removes any unevennesses which may have occurred while the balls of clay lay waiting to be used.

129 The action can be quite fast. The top should be convex before upward squeezing begins or it may develop a deep concavity.

130 Some inward pressure is needed while the clay is being forced down otherwise it may mushroom out uncontrollably or simply trap air at the base of the clay lump. During the whole upward and downward motion the clay may though round and centred be revolving on a different axis to the wheel. If the clay was suddenly released it would show a considerable sway. Pressure should always be released gradually when the hands are removed from the clay at any stage of throwing. This allows the clay to settle in a centred position.

131 The clay is pushed down until its height and width are roughly equal before the next stage of throwing proceeds. The next step is to open up the centred ball of clay. There are two common ways of doing this.

132

133

134

135

In both these actions the outside of the clay is supported as the inside is opened up. In both the initial hole is not vertical but at an angle so the inside can be seen and the thickness of the base left by the opening up be seen as well as felt. With practice opening up should become a single smooth action creating a base of the intended thickness and width.

Once the clay has been opened up a first action for a beginner, simply to understand the process and to get the initial feel of clay as it is being thinned, could be to grip the wall with the thumb of the right hand inside and the fingers outside and while gripping to move the hand steadily from the base of the wall to the edge. Obviously the forms that can be made one handed are very limited in scale but the point of a beginner doing this is to get the feel of the action.

Once initial attempts have been made the first aim should be to throw cylinders with as even walls as possible in no more than three upward movements. One should be quite precise about which parts of the fingers are doing the work. The whole principle is that the revolving clay is passed between two points of pressure which move evenly upwards. Throughout throwing it is important that the hands and the clay are well lubricated with water and it should be water not slip certainly for beginners otherwise the surface can become very messy. Slip will build up on the hands during throwing but, especially as each form is finished, the build up should be removed. In each of the three upward movements pressure should begin right at the bottom and proceed evenly to the top. The hands should not spiral off the top of the pot but should momentarily steady it and each time should begin the intended form of the finished edge.

136 137 138 The first upward movement

139

140

141

The second upward movement

142

143

144

145

The third upward movement
The final throwing action is to finish the edge.

A beginner should practice this until it can be done with some confidence. Before they are put aside to be reprepared the cylinders should be cut up to show the base and wall section. When some degree of confidence has been achieved it should be possible to produce cylinders of the same width and the same height from identical amounts of clay.

As well as cutting up the cylinders to see the wall section three actions can be practised. The surplus clay at the bottom of the outside of the thrown wall can be trimmed off with a pointed wooden or metal tool. As well as being done at the end of throwing this can also be done before the final thinning action. The top edge can be trimmed with a needle or wire. If clay preparation was thoroughly done and if throwing was alright no evenness should develop in the top edge but unevennesses do develop and it is useful to be able to deal with them. Either a needle safely set into a cork is pushed through the wall about 6 mm from the top to the hand on the inside or a wire held tautly between the top index fingers is dropped down into the top edge. When the wheel, going at a medium speed, has revolved a few times the top edge will start to move and separate itself. If, at this stage, the hands are lifted clear of the pot the complete top edge will be removed. The third thing to practise, even if throwing bats are available, is lifting pots off the wheel. The pot is cut off the wheel with a thin wire or nylon thread. This can be done with the wheel revolving slowly, or stationary, in both cases the wire is firmly held down as it is passed under the pot. There are countless variations of cutting off; some use a twisted wire, which can produce a shallow spiral relief on the base; some have the wheel revolving; some cut through water, some cut dry; some lift with dry hands, some with wet. Experiments should be made until a preferred method is found but it is important that the attempt to lift pots off the wheel is made right from the beginning. Whatever else is done the lifting action requires a firm, gentle pressure.

146

Throwing bowl forms is a slightly different process to throwing cylinders. Bowls usually have a curved inside shape of one sort or another so an important visible part of the bowl is made at the stage of opening up. Bowls are invariably turned when leather hard (see pages 96 to 100), so the thrown exterior form is not seen at the throwing stage as it is with more cylindrical forms.

It must be emphasised that bowls cannot be thrown on a very fast wheel. The wider the bowl the slower the wheel needs to be. A bowl that begins to wobble has generally begun to collapse near its base. Attempting to steady such a bowl by collaring – moving both hands up the outside which might effectively steady a cylinder – is useless.

The edge of any pot is important but bowls have more and more obvious edge than other thrown forms.

147
148

The first thinning action should not bring the wall out too shallow and should only begin when the unthrown, supported base of the bowl has been established. Any real adjustment to the curve of the base of the bowl should not be done after this first thinning action. An uninterrupted continuity of curve between the supported base and the thrown wall should be established at this stage.

The second thinning action can make the bowl shallower. Care should be taken now and in subsequent thinning and shaping actions not to allow a bump to develop at the point where the supported base becomes the thrown wall. If the edge of the bowl is kept slightly inward turning this will help the steadiness of the bowl.

149

150 The final thinning action should establish fairly exactly the basic form of the bowl and does determine the limits to which the final form can develop. It is not possible to make bowls less shallow once they have been thinned. Sometimes, especially with larger bowls, more than three thinning actions will be necessary but the quicker the thinness wanted can be achieved then the more time can be given to any necessary alterations to the form or finishing of the edge.

If the problem of a bump forming between the supported base and the thrown wall is encountered what is happening is that at the point where the thrown wall begins too great a pressure is being exerted from the inside. On larger bowls some throwers prefer to work with the right hand inside until the point where a bump could occur has been passed and then to revert to the usual left hand inside position.

The last illustration clearly shows the relative position of the hands during the throwing of open forms.

Most vertical forms are developed from roughly cylindrical beginnings but with very full spherical forms the form should be established from early stages.

151 The first thinning action begins to determine the form – though at this stage nothing in detail is determined about the final form.

152 At the end of the second movement the limits of the final nature of the form have begun to be determined.

153 If necessary any surplus clay should be trimmed from the base at this stage. This does not of course prevent further clay being trimmed at the end.

154 The third thinning should use as much as practicable of the available clay right from the base.

155

One or more shaping movement should be easily possible if the clay has been evenly thrown to its thinness in a rèasonable time. These shaping actions do not affect the thinness of the walls. Possible shaping, on the whole, is only into fuller, wider shapes.

In the last two illustrations the relative positions of the hands during thinning and shaping are clear. In the widening lower parts of the form the effective fingers of the right hand are somewhat below those of the left hand inside. In the narrowing parts of the upper part the effective fingers of the right hand are above those of the left hand.

The emphasis on three thinning actions in previous pages should not be misunderstood. It may be that on a small scale two movements from bottom to top of the pot thin it effectively and on a large scale quite a few additional movements may be necessary. The essential thing is that the thinning is always done as efficiently as possible. The quicker it can be done the more time is available for consideration of and adjustment to the final form and details of the pot.

156

Clearly the edge of a thrown pot affects its overall visual appearance very considerably. Edges always need careful consideration and in cases where they are large or of very specific form they need to be allowed for from the very first thinning movement otherwise sufficient clay will not be available. There is a very large variety of possible lid seating some requiring specific treatment to the pot edge others to the lid edge and others to both. Calipers for measuring are essential when lids are being thrown.

Thrown spouts, such as are found on many thrown teapots, are made by collaring small conical or cylindrical forms. Collaring which can be done on a larger scale as well is simply squeezing the outside of the thrown walls and moving the hands upwards. When the body of a bottle form has been thrown the top is collared in and thinned in alternate actions. Likewise, but on this scale it is probably done only with the index finger and thumb of both hands, thrown teapot spouts are shaped by collaring. All very narrow topped forms can be altered and even thinned by using a narrow tool to reach the inside of the walls. With teapot spouts a small round brush handle does the job effectively.

Throwing ribs are shaped wooden or fired clay tools which are used sometimes in the later thinning stages but usually in the shaping stages. They produce a precise sort of line and eliminate the spiral ridges which the fingers leave during throwing. Ribs are not templates in that they are moved over the surface of the pot just as the hands are. Templates can be used in throwing. Their use is usually limited to the making of beadings at the top of a pot but they can be and have been used to form the complete profile of pots.

As well as being done directly onto a wheelhead throwing can be done on removable bats made of plaster, asbestos or wood (marine ply). Bats, obviously, greatly facilitate the removal of large or thinly thrown pots from the wheel. Bats made of plaster, asbestos or wood can be secured to the wheel by suction if they are placed onto a thin ridged layer of clay thrown thinly across the wheelhead. Bats made of asbestos or wood can be drilled with two holes, one in the centre and one a precise distance from it, which locate the bat by means of pegs fixed into the wheelhead.

As well as being done directly onto a wheelhead or bat throwing can be done from the top of a centred hump of clay. The process has definite limits of scale but can be very useful for the throwing of most small forms and especially some lids.

The throwing of many shapes of the same shape and size – repeat throwing – is demanding for the beginner but it is a discipline through which a precision of control can be achieved. It is wrong to think of it as a very mechanical process and to attempt to check too many measurements with calipers and height gauges. Perhaps the best mechanical aid is a soft brush or the soft end of a quill stuck into a lump of clay so that its soft end just misses the edge of the pot. If this aid and a single prototype on the wheel ledge are the starting point the aim should be to achieve the similarity of form by eye and by a similarity of rhythm of motion in the throwing. Repeat throwing is pointless if results are tired and lifeless and they are, ironically, most likely to be this if exactness of repetition is the aim. It is far more important to create a similarity of feeling from pot to pot and this comes far more from a rhythm of work than from concern for exactitude. A sufficient degree of measurable similarity will come with practice but it is only worth achieving this if the quality of form is not lost in the process.

The speed of revolution of a wheel during throwing is important. Generally speaking the making of thrown objects is accompanied by a gradual decrease in the speed of the wheel: the wheel revolves fastest during centering and slowest when the walls are thinnest, during the final stages of finishing. The actual speed of rotation depends on the nature of the clay being used, the softness of the clay, the size of the thrown pot, its form, its width and, importantly, on the preference of the thrower. Beginners learning on electric wheels frequently experience difficulty because they forget to slow down the wheel as the throwing proceeds.

Many types of wheels are now available and all have their advocates. Kick wheels come in direct flywheel kick, side treadle kick, and front treadle kick. Front treadle kick are just about serviceable for turning but should be avoided for throwing for which they are very poor. Electric wheels come as variable speed motor drive or constant speed motor, mechanically variable drive. Good electric and kick wheels are available or can be made. A wheel is only a tool and the final decision about which is best is only the preference of each individual. The one basic difference is that with an electric wheel a competent thrower can do whatever is possible for one individual to do whereas with a kick wheel, even one with a very heavy flywheel, a competent thrower may need an assistant to kick the wheel if he is throwing very tall pots.

As well as throwing pots from a single piece of clay it is also possible to build up larger forms by throwing in stages. Narrow forms can be made by adding bottomless, thick, centred forms to the top of previously thrown forms and by throwing the new clay wall up from the old. Forms can be made by assembling thrown elements top edge to top edge – this can be done both with and without rethrowing the top form but usually involves the rethrowing and widening of the top form and was the traditional way of making large water containers – it is still used in some Mediterranean countries and is done in two, three or more stages. Or forms can be made progressively by coiling and throwing – a fat coil is added to the top edge of a thrown form and is centred and thrown upwards, when this edge has dried a new coil can be added and so on. All three of these processes allow larger forms to be thrown than could be made from one piece of clay and all three allow slightly different possibilities.

TURNING

In pottery the term turning can refer to three different processes. It can be used to describe the forming of a plaster or clay shape on a lathe or wheel as a model for a moulding process. It can refer, in the process known as *throwing and turning*, to the final shaping and detailing of a hollow clay vessel. It can also refer to the trimming and partial shaping of a thrown form. The first use of the term is not of concern in the present context.

In throwing and turning forms are thickly but evenly thrown greater attention being given to the finish and shape of the inside rather than the outside. The entire outside surface of the form is subsequently turned. Throwing and turning as a mass production process exploited (and, in so far as it is still done to a small extent, exploits) those qualities that are peculiar to turning – smoothness, precision, and, most particularly, turned beadings. Mouldings can never reproduce the fineness or elaborateness of the horizontal beadings of turned forms. Use of the technique was at its height in Western Europe in the eighteenth century.

The process of throwing is fundamentally different to that of turning. In throwing forms are made and modified by manipulative, plastic means; in turning forms are made and modified by reduction, by paring away layers of clay from an already made and rigid form. The different qualities which are inherent in the two processes are clear if a thrown and turned pot and a thrown pot are placed side by side. A very frequent context for turning however is in a thrown pot or bowl which needs trimming. The problem with this process is not a technical one but a visual one. The problem is to turn a form as much as is needed and to do it sympathetically. Thrown qualities and turned qualities are not irreconcilable but where the two processes are used together it is important that the resultant qualities do relate to each other.

Probably the most frequent context of turning is the base of bowl forms. Forms which are to be turned should be carefully watched as they dry. Thrown pots dry at their edges first and if left right way up bowls may well be too dry to be safely supported on or by their edge when the base is at the right consistency for turning. Bowls and other forms which are to be turned on the base should therefore be placed upside down as soon as is practicable so the base can dry out and the drying of the top can be retarded.

157 Though it is neither practicable or good as a method where considerable production occurs most bowl forms can be safely attached to the wheel-head for turning with small coils of clay carefully pressed round the edge. The first action in turning the base of any pot is to remove the obvious flange of unwanted clay.

158 The clay should be firm enough to be pared away cleanly and should be soft enough to do so in longish strands. If the clay burrs up it is too soft; if it comes away in a shower of little dry pieces it is too hard.

159 Only when the exterior profile has been completed should the inside of the foot be turned away. To do so earlier would obviously restrict the extent or nature of the exterior curve.

160 The surest way of knowing the thickness of a pot as it is being turned is to look at it and feel it prior to turning and to remember it. This works as long as there is a fixed known point, which most conveniently is the unturned base. The last turning therefore should be to the edge of the foot ring.

161 With grogged clays turning can make rough abrasive surfaces. The base of a foot ring should therefore always be finally smoothed with a wooden tool held at a shallow angle to push the grog into the clay.

Most shapes of pot can be held on the wheel in one or other of two basic forms of chuck. When centred and well seated on or in a chuck pots being turned should stay in position without any other support providing both pot and chuck are the right consistency – a little on the soft side of leather hard. Metal cup heads, for jigger and jolley work, lined with a thick coil of clay turned to accommodate the pot being turned make workable substitutes for clay chucks.

Open shapes are placed over a convex sided chuck. With practice shapes can be placed on to and removed from chucks with the wheel still revolving.

162 Until that point of confidence has been reached it is safer to place the pot on to the stationary chuck.

163 It is then centred, if adjustment is necessary, by a slight pressure on the edge of the base where the eccentricity will be greatest. The form should almost click on to centre when the movement is mastered.

164 Turning then proceeds.

165 More enclosed shapes are placed in the top of a hollow chuck with an inward sloping broad edge.

166 The form is centred as the wheel begins to revolve.

167 Turning proceeds.

The condition of tools is more important than might seem when the relative softness of clay is considered. Turning tools should be kept sharp. Stainless steel tools though they have the obvious advantage of not rusting are difficult to sharpen to a good edge and in many ways ordinary steel turning tools are preferable. Bent packing case wire makes excellent turning tools. Tools should never be sharpened where there is any chance of the filings getting into the clay.

168 A metal kidney can be a useful turning tool where smooth and continuous curves and surfaces are wanted.

MAKING SPOUTS ON THROWN POTS

Pouring spouts on thrown pots have taken and can take a wide variety of forms. Basically there are two alternatives, the spout can be shaped out of the top edge of the pot while it is still damp as with most thrown jugs or it can be made as a separate form and attached to the main body of the vessel at the leather-hard state as with most thrown teapots. Making teapot spouts is simply making precise thrown forms, the complexity of the process is relating the separate units to each other. Making pulled spouts on jugs is a very much more direct process and permits great variety.

169 The first finger and thumb of one hand define the width of the spout and push the edge in slightly or at least hold it steady.

170 The edge is stroked outwards progressively. The extent to which an up and down motion inside the edge of the jug is necessary is determined by the form of the jug. Some forms need a well defined channel to pour efficiently, some do not.

171 After the spout has been initially pulled its form can be modified by gentle pushing from the outside. The efficiency of a spout is determined to some extent by the actual edge of the thrown form.

172 A final action is often to bend over the very edge of the spout. A variation to the above process is to pinch the wall in which the spout is pulled. This can give a fuller, more generous curve to the spout.

173 Pinching is done in the wall below the edge and usually aims to raise the edge at the two extremities of the spout. When pinching does go right to the edge it usually only affects the two points which define the ends of the spout.

174 The spout is pulled quite normally. The pinching gives it a curve upwards towards the spout. Pinching can be considerable and can affect the line of the top very extensively.

175 Pouring can be assisted by a vertical channel beneath the spout. This can be put in a variety of ways and may be done before or after the spout edge is pulled.

All actions in the pulling of spouts and the making of channels should be flowing and should not be slow otherwise the result can become tired and overworked.

HANDLES

Traditionally thrown pots usually had pulled handles and turned pots had extruded or moulded (either slip cast or press moulded) handles.

Extruded handles are made in a wad-box which is a simple hand-operated machine consisting of a metal cylinder down which a metal plunger can be wound. At the base of the cylinder is a flange on which the dies rest. As the plunger is wound down the clay in the cylinder is forced through the die which produces a continuous strip of handle. The dies are drilled and filed by hand to produce handle strips of whatever is the desired cross-section. Extruded handles, obviously, are without taper. Certain specific types of handles are thrown.

The process of pulling a handle has some similarities with throwing: the hands and clay are lubricated with water; the pressures involved are similar; the importance of clay preparation is vital.

It is a much better idea to pull handles near a bucket of water rather than over a sink. Pieces of clay will inevitably and intentionally be pinched off the ends of handles and whole handles will be scrapped. If this occurs on a sink and draining board it can make a troublesome mess whereas working on a bench the clay can be put on one side and the slip and water allowed to fall into the bucket.

There are two processes related to the pulling of handles but they are very similar. A handle can be pulled and subsequently attached to a pot or clay can be attached to a pot and a handle pulled from this. The visual and practical difference between the two processes is slight. Which process is used is largely a matter of preference.

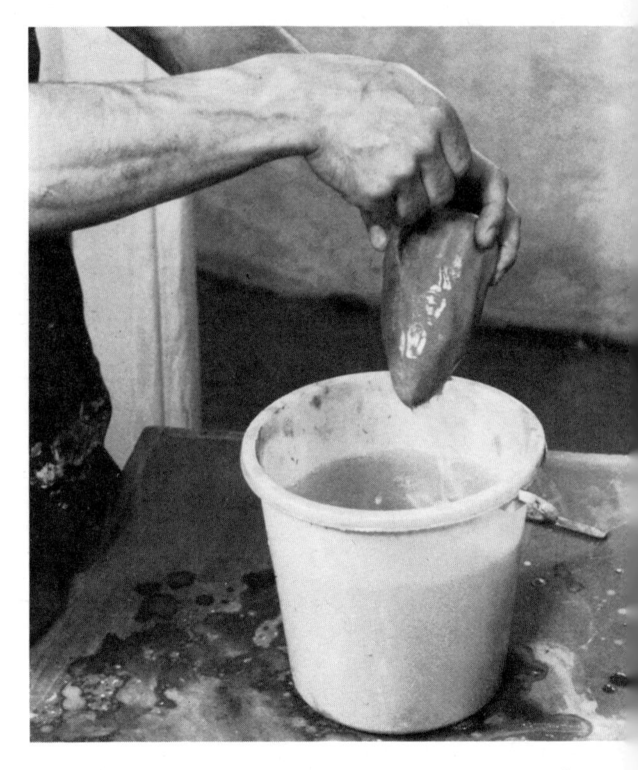

176 When pulling handles for subsequent attachment a lump of well prepared clay is beaten into an even and roughly conical shape, is firmly held at the top and is wetted.

177 The first action – squeezing from near the top and moving the hand towards the bottom – is rather like centring and should give the lump an even end from which the handle can be pulled.

178 Once pulling has begun the handle should be held and pulled vertically so that the strip is an even one both the left hand and the right should turn as necessary so that symetry is maintained as much as is wanted. (Not all handles may have to be even from side to side, for example pulled handles attached horizontally to the side of pots may be much thicker on one side than the other.)

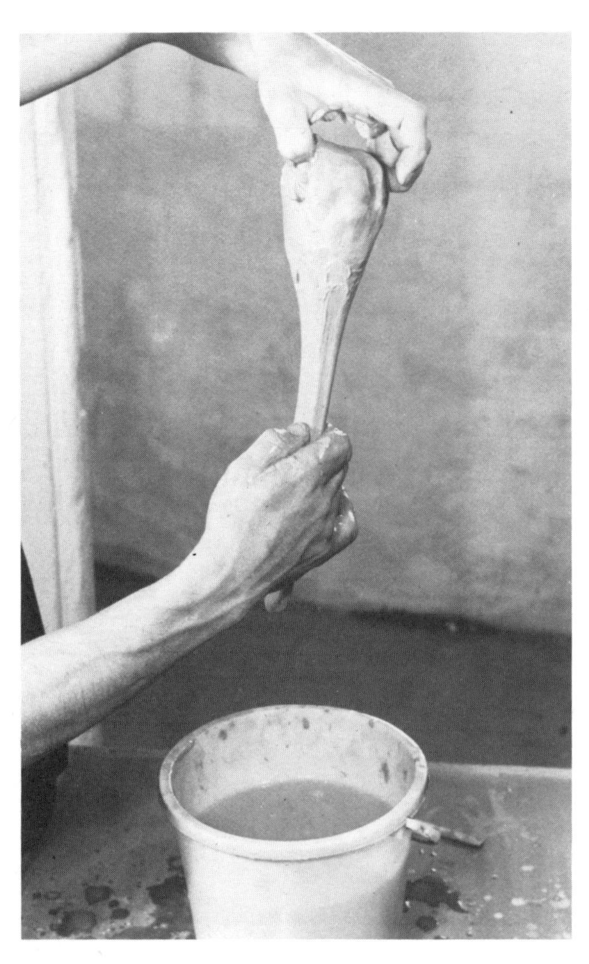

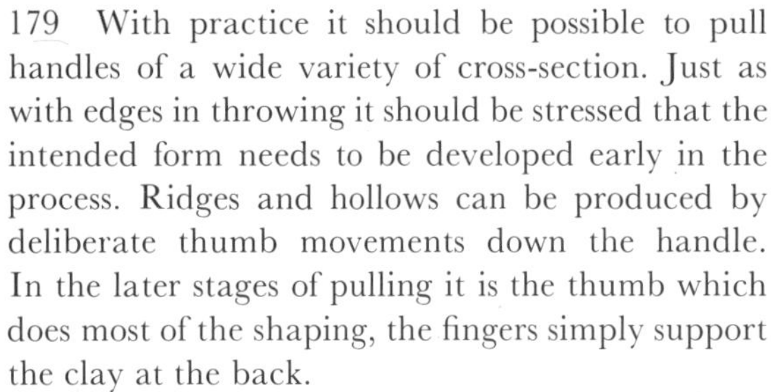

179 With practice it should be possible to pull handles of a wide variety of cross-section. Just as with edges in throwing it should be stressed that the intended form needs to be developed early in the process. Ridges and hollows can be produced by deliberate thumb movements down the handle. In the later stages of pulling it is the thumb which does most of the shaping, the fingers simply support the clay at the back.

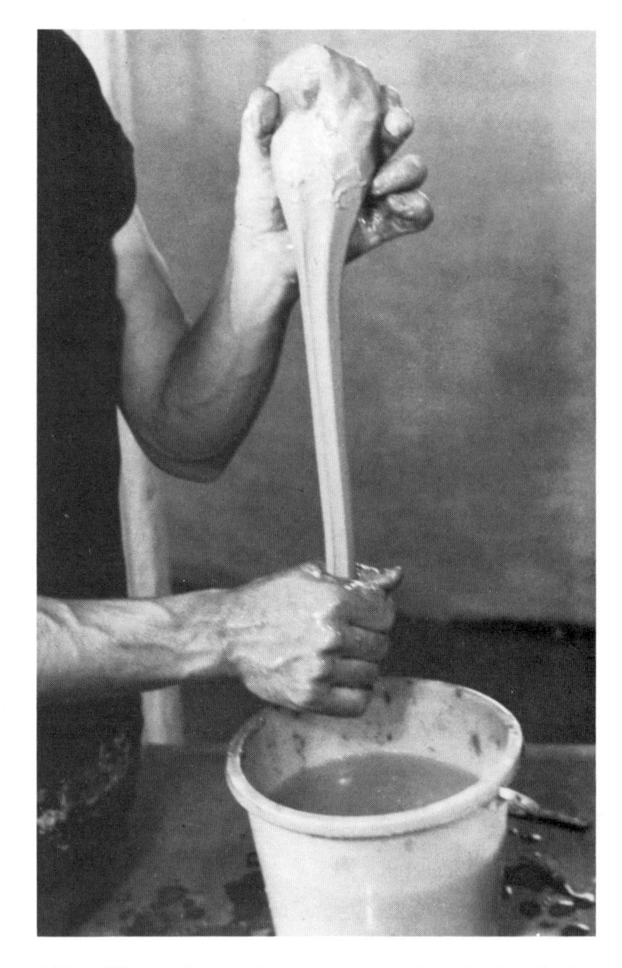

180 Throughout the process the hands should be wet – just as in throwing – and slip which builds up on the hands should be washed off. It is quite unnecessary though to keep dipping the hands into water. The last action is very gentle and usually intends to soften any unwanted sharpnesses left by the thumb and to remove slip from the surface. When pulled the handle is attached by 25 mm or more of clay above the intended top edge of the handle hanging over the edge of a board and is left to stiffen a little.

Handles should not be allowed to get too firm before being attached. The clay should still be plastic and without any tendency to crack when bent.

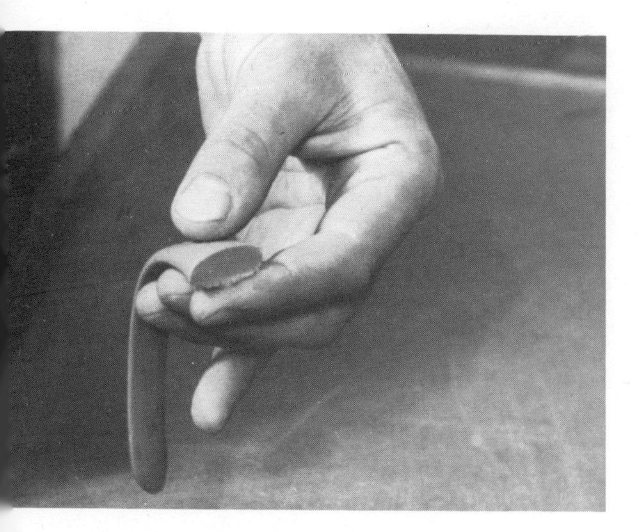

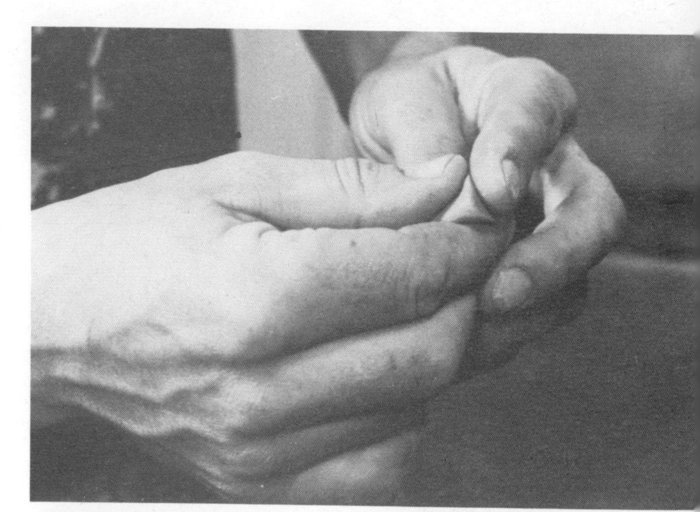

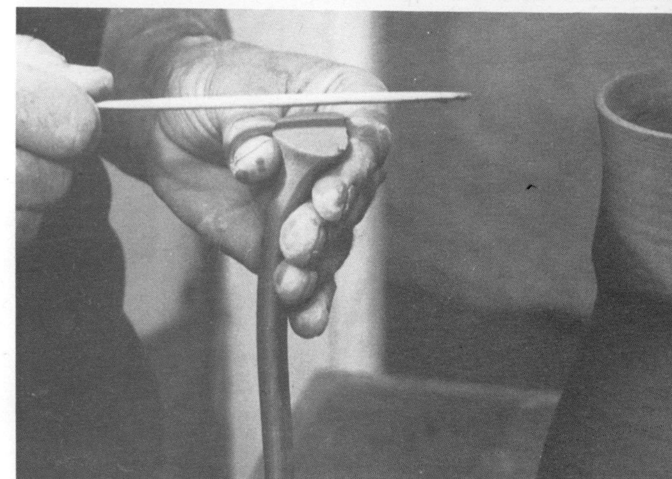

181 The handle is cut at the appropriate angle.

182

183 The end is pressed or tapped to produce somè clay which can be smoothed into the pot.

There are a number of different ways of attaching the clay of the handle to the clay of the pot. The area of attachment on the pot can be scratched and be smeared with slip or it can be scratched and sponged with water to produce slip or slip can be applied or just a little water can be rubbed around with a finger. Which method is used is a matter partly of preference but also a matter of knowledge of a particular clay – some clays join up readily, others are much more difficult. Whichever method is used the procedure for attachment is the same and does not alter with scale.

184 The handle is pressed on to the pot which makes the join.

185

186

The ridge of clay is smoothed into the pot around the handle to complete the join.

187

188

The lower end is only fixed when the join of the upper end is complete. The handle forms its own curve. Sometimes pulled handles are called sprung handles. If it is necessary to alter the curve of the handle this can be done by running a wet finger on the inside of the handle pushing gently outwards.

189
190

191 The actual nature of the join of the bottom is very important. An area of the handle is attached. The tendency to push through the soft end of the handle and leave very little area of attachment must be avoided. The thickness of the area may of course be tapered without affecting its strength. It should also be said that it is perfectly possible to attach handles at the top as well as the bottom by this process rather than the more right-angled one described.

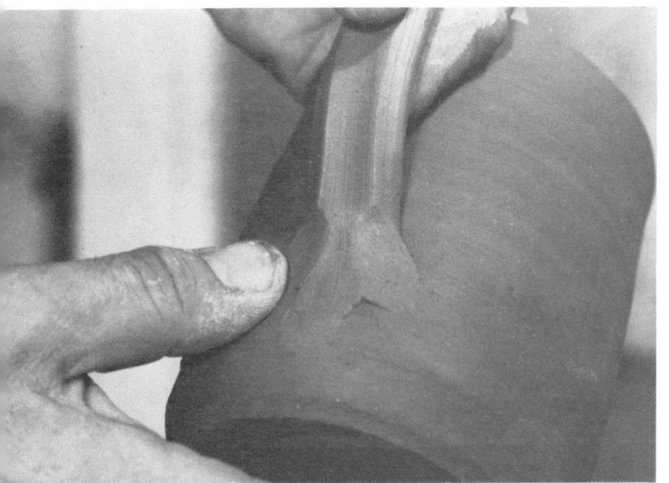

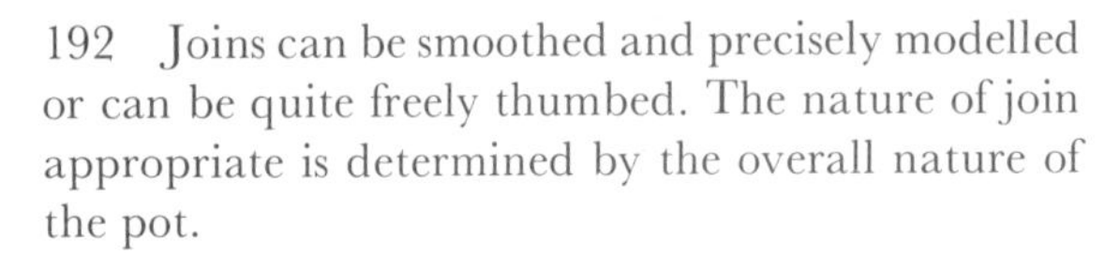

192 Joins can be smoothed and precisely modelled or can be quite freely thumbed. The nature of join appropriate is determined by the overall nature of the pot.

193 The crevice produced between the handle and the pot and the bottom join of most handles can be filled in by the addition of a small coil which is smoothed into the pot and handle.

194 195 Pulled handles can be applied hori zontally as lugs.

Pulling handles directly on a pot is not very different to pulling them separately but it is probably as well to be able to pull handles from a lump of clay with confidence before pulling on a pot is attempted.

196 197 198 199

The first step is to firmly fix, by the preferred and appropriate method, a piece of clay of appropriate size and shape. This can usually be smaller than one imagines.

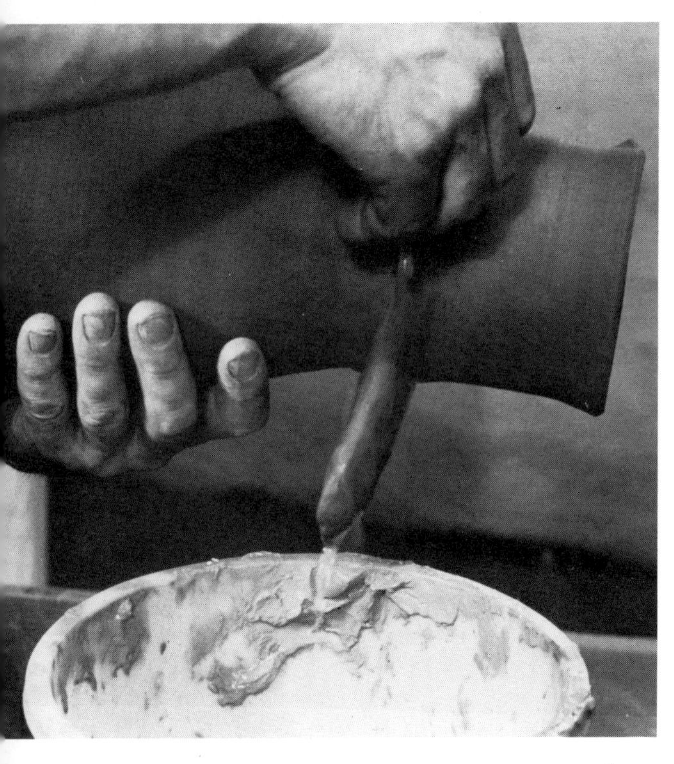

200 Once fixed and pinched to an even shape the hands, or with larger handles, the clay and the hands can be wetted.

201 202

The handle can then be pulled. It should be pulled right from the join otherwise the join might be left excessively thick. Pulling can have just as much control of detail as when done from a lump.

203

204

205 The lower end is joined as soon as pulling is finished. In that the clay is pulled from a strip rather than a lump of clay it gets comparatively less wet than when pulling from a lump so sagging should not be a problem.

With large pots handles may have thumb stops added or a small lug may be applied on the opposite side to the handle at the base to facilitate lifting when pouring.

Section Three The nature of pottery materials: the firing process

LIST OF MATERIALS USED IN POTTERY

	Name	*Formula*	*Unit Weight*	*Other name or names*	*Notes*
1	Alabaster	$CaSO_42H_2O$	172	Calcium sulphate or Gypsum	The raw material of plaster of paris (see Gypsum)
2	Alumina	Al_2O_3	102	Oxide of aluminium	An important ingredient in all clays and glazes
3	Albite	$Na_2OAl_2O_36SiO_2$	526	Soda felspar	
4	Anorthite	$CaOAl_2O_32SiO_2$	278	Lime felspar	
5	Antimoniate of lead	—	—	—	Composition variable. A yellow pigment only stable in lead glazes
6	Barium carbonate	$BaCO_3$	197	—	Similar to calcium carbonate which it could replace in glazes. Used especially in matt glazes. Up to 2½% used in red earthenware bodies to prevent white scumming
7	Barium sulphate	$BaSO_4$	233	Barytes	Used like barium carbonate to prevent scumming
8	Bentonite	—	—	—	Exceptionally plastic clay
9	Bone ash	$Ca_3(PO_4)_2$	310	Calcium phosphate	A basic fluxing ingredient that promotes translucency in bone china
10	Boric acid	H_3BO_3	—	Boracic acid	Used in frits as a source of boric oxide when soda is not required
11	Boric oxide	B_2O_3	70	Oxide of boron	Acid ingredient used in soft glazes usually in the form of borax
12	Borax (calcined)	$Na_2B_4O_7$	202	Sodium diborate	Useful in soft glazes as it introduces both sodium and boric oxides
13	Borocalcite	$CaO_2B_2O_36H_2O$	304	Colemanite	Used in soft glazes. Introduces both calcium and boric oxides
14	Calcium oxide	CaO	56	Lime (Quicklime)	Not used in this form because it is corrosive and unstable
15	Calcium carbonate	$CaCO_3$	100	Carbonate of lime	Occurs naturally as marble, chalk, limestone, whiting
16	China clay	$Al_2O_32SiO_22H_2O$	258	Kaolin	Purest form of clay. White. Sedimentary (see Clay substance)
17	Chromium sesquioxide	Cr_2O_3	152	Green oxide of chrome; Chrome oxide	Useful colouring pigment giving a range of colours in different contexts: reds, yellows, pinks and greens
18	Chromate of potash	$K_2Cr_2O_7$	294	Potassium dichromate	An alternative source of chrome oxide used in frits and in calcined colours

	Name	Formula	Unit Weight	Other name or names	Notes
19	Clay substance	$Al_2O_32SiO_22H_2O$	258	—	Hypothetical 'ideal' clay. Most clays conform to this formula but have varying amounts of additional sand, iron, lime, vegetable matter, etc
20	Cobaltous oxide	CoO	75	Cobalt oxide	A very stable pigment giving blues. A strong flux
21	Cobalt carbonate	$CoCO_3$	119	—	A very stable pigment giving blues slightly less strong in tone than cobalt oxide
22	Copper oxide (black)	CuO	79	Cupric oxide	Colouring pigments giving a wide range of colours, greens, blues, reds, etc according to the kind of glaze and firing (22–24)
23	Copper oxide (red)	Cu_2O	143	Cuprous oxide	
24	Copper carbonate (basic)	$CuCO_3CuOH_2$	221	One of several salts of copper	
25	Cornish Stone, purple 0·012 MgO 0·157 CaO 0·340 K_2O 0·244 Na_2O	$Al_2O_36{\cdot}82SiO_2$	569	Pegmatite, China stone	A natural rock of variable composition. One of the matrix rocks of clay. It is a mixture of felspar with quartz and mica. The white stone is the more refractory (25–26)
26	Cornish stone, white 0·048 MgO 0·204 CaO 0·280 K_2O 0·040 Na_2O	$Al_2O_37{\cdot}5SiO_2$	594	Pegmatite, China stone	
27	Cristobalite	SiO_2	60	Crystalline silica	A type of crystalline silica formed at a stage in the firing cycle
28	Crocus martis	—	—	—	Impure ferric oxide with some nitrate additions
29	Cryolite	Al_33NaF	210	Sodium Aluminium Fluoride	Provides a natural and unfritted form of sodium. Reduces crazing in glazes. Fluoride content can, because of volatilisation, lead to pinholing and pitting of glaze
30	Fluorspar	CaF_2	78	Calcium Fluoride, Derbyshire spar	A strong flux. Source in glazes of calcium. Fluorine content can, because of volatilisation, lead to pinholing and pitting of glaze
31	Dolomite	$CaMg(CO_3)_2$	200	Calcium magnesium carbonate	Useful as a flux in stoneware glazes
32	Felspar	$Na_2OAl_2O_36SiO_2$	524	Albite, Soda felspar	A natural rock of variable composition. These four are the types most commonly used in
		$CaOAl_2O_32SiO_2$	278	Anorthite, Lime felspar	
		$K_2O3Na_2O4Al_2O_38SiO_2$	761	Nepheline Syenite	
		$K_2OAl_2O_36SiO_2$	556	Orthoclase, Potash felspar	
33	Ferric oxide	Fe_2O_3	160	Red oxide of iron	The most usual iron oxide: it occurs in many clays and is used as a colouring pigment. Several types exist

	Name	Formula	Unit Weight	Other name or names	Notes
34	Ferrous oxide	FeO	72	Unstable oxide of iron	Ferric oxide changes to ferrous oxide in reducing conditions during firing
35	Ferroso-ferric oxide	Fe_3O_4	232/3	Magnetite; Black iron oxide, magnetic	Produces spotty effect when used in glazes
36	Ferrous sulphide	FeS_2	120	Iron pyrites	Sometimes in clays and is harmful, causing black spots and 'spit outs'
37	Flint	SiO_2	60	Crypto-crystalline silica	Flint pebbles when calcined and ground are used both in bodies and glazes
38	Galena			Lead sulphide	See lead sulphide
39	Gold chloride	$AuCl_3$		Auric chloride	A gold salt; the most usual form of gold for use on pottery
40	Granite	—	—	—	Rock composed of felspar, quartz, etc. Cornish stone is a type of granite
41	Gypsum	—	—	Alabaster	See Alabaster
42	Haematite	Fe_2O_3	160	One type of ferric oxide	See Ferric oxide. Haematite will take a high polish if burnished
43	Ilmenite	$FeOTiO_2$	152	Ferrous titanate	Used in glazes to obtain speckled effects
44	Iron chromate	$Fe_2O_3Cr_2O_3$	312		
45	Kaolin	—	—	China clay	See China clay
46	Kieselguhr	SiO_2	60	Amorphous silica	Diatomaceous earth used for insulation of kilns. Relatively it is very light
47	Lepidolite	—	—	—	A source of lithium for use in high temperature glazes. Its fluourine content can cause pitting or pinholing through volatilisation. See also Petalite which contains no fluorine
48	Lead sulphide	PbS	239	Galena, blacklead	These types of raw lead can all be used in glazes but they are a serious health hazard if not carefully used and their use is now forbidden in most educational contexts and in the industry where fritted leads may be used
49	Lead oxide	PbO	223	Litharge	
50	Lead carbonate	$PbCO_3$	267	White lead	
51	Lead Peroxide	Pb_3O_4	685	Red lead	
52	Lead monosilicate	$PbSiO_3$	283	Fritted lead	Frits formed by fritting some form of raw lead with silica. These frits minimise, but do not entirely remove the dangers, inherent in lead glazing and glazes
53	Lead bisilicate	PbO_2SiO_2	343	Fritted lead	
54	Lead sesquisilicate	$PbO1{\cdot}5SiO_2$	313	Fritted lead	
55	Magnesium oxide	MgO	40		A flux in glazes. The usual source for this is magnesium carbonate or dolomite
56	Magnesium carbonate	$MgCO_3$	84		A source of magnesium oxide used in high temperature glazes. Tends to give a mattness to glazes

	Name	Formula	Unit Weight	Other name or names	Notes
57	Manganese carbonate	$MgCO_3$	115		Colouring pigments giving colours in the brown range in lead glazes and in the purple range in alkaline glazes
58	Manganese dioxide	MnO_2	87		
59	Mica	—	—	A hydrous silicate	One of a group of silicates rather similar to clay. Has a laminated structure
60	Nepheline Syenite	—	—	A form of felspar	See felspar
61	Nickel oxide	NiO	75		A colouring pigment giving greys and greens
62	Petalite	$Li_2OAl_2O_38SiO_2$	584		A natural source of lithium. Used as a secondary flux in high temperature glazes
63	Platinic chloride	$PtCl_5H_2O$	427	Chloride of platinum	Salt of platinum providing a silver-coloured pigment for on-glaze work
64	Potassium Bichromate	$K_2Cr_2O_7$	294		Soluble and poisonous. Used in the preparation of calcined ceramic colours
65	Potassium carbonate	K_2CO_3	138	Pearl ash	Soluble sources of potassium. Usually fritted for use in glazes
66	Potassium nitrate	KNO_3	101	Nitre	
67	Potassium oxide	K_2O	94		
68	Quartz	SiO_2	60		Alternative to flint in bodies and glazes
69	Rutile	—	—		Naturally occurring ores containing titanium and iron oxides in varying proportions. Used to create speckled effects in glazes
70	Salt	NaCl	58	Sodium chloride	Used in salt glazing
71	Sand			Silica	See Silica
72	Selenium	Se	79		Oxides of this are a source of red in glass and low fired glazes
73	Silica	SiO_2	60	Silicon dioxide	Occurs naturally in various forms – sand, flint, quarts – and as an ingredient in clay and many rocks
74	Silicon carbide	SiC	40		Used occasionally in glazes to induce localised reduction. It is used as a refractory material, as an electric element material and as an abrasive
75	Sodium carbonate (anhydrous)	Na_2CO_3	106	Soda ash	Basic ingredient in glazes. It is soluble and is usually fritted. Soda ash is also used as a deflocculent in casting slips
76	Sodium oxide	Na_2O	62	Caustic soda	Dangerously caustic when dissolved in water. Unstable. Not suitable unfritted for use in pottery

	Name	Formula	Unit Weight	Other name or names	Notes
77	Sodium silicate	—	—	Water glass	Composition variable. Used as a deflocculent in casting slips. Two viscosities are normally available 75° or 150° Twaddell
78	Stannic oxide	SnO_2	151	Tin oxide	A white pigment. Used to opacify glazes
79	Strontium carbonate	$SrCO_3$	148		A flux in glazes
80	Talc	—	—	French chalk, Hydrated magnesium silicate	Composition variable. Used as a flux in glazes and bodies. Sometimes dusted onto plaster moulds to facilitate release of slip casts
81	Tin oxide	SnO_3	151	Stannic oxide	See stannic oxide
82	Titanium dioxide	TiO_2	80		Used as a creamy coloured opacifier in glazes
83	Whiting	$CaCO_3$	100	Calcium carbonate	See Calcium carbonate
84	Zinc oxide	ZnO	81		A useful auxiliary flux in glazes. Has a matting effect and used to excess can lead to pinholing or promote crawling
85	Zirconium oxide	ZrO_2	122	Zirconia	Used in glazes as opacifiers. Also used in the manufacture of pottery colours and special high temperature bodies and refractories
86	Zirconium silicate	$ZrSiO_4$	182	Zircon	(as above)

THE CHEMISTRY OF POTTERY MATERIALS

For those who may be daunted by the idea that a knowledge of chemistry is a prerequisite for the making of pottery it must be categorically stated that it is not. Empirical experiment with bought or found materials can be applied. Bought prepared glazes and colours can be used. The visual and functional quality of an object depends on how materials are used not so much on precisely what is used. The advantage of understanding something of the chemistry of pottery materials is important not as an end in itself but because it can make the process of experiment more certain and less time-consuming. The principles involved are relatively simple and once even a limited understanding has been achieved much that might have previously seemed daunting can be done simply and quickly.

The definitions of chemical terms which follow will be known by all with a knowledge of simple chemistry.

Element

> 'A substance which, so far as we know, contains only one kind of matter.' *Mellor*

Most substances have a natural affinity for some other substances and, in nature, elements are rarely found in elemental form but are combined with other elements.

Atom

> 'An atom is the unit of chemical exchange . . . the smallest part of an element that can take part in a chemical reaction.' *Mellor*

Molecule

'The smallest part of an element or compound that can exist in a free state.' *Mellor*

Chemical compound

A chemical compound consists of two or more elements combined chemically in definite proportions by weight.

A mixture

A mixture occurs when elements or compounds exist side by side without forming a new substance. Mixtures do not have definite proportions of ingredients by weight.

A solution

A solution is a homogenous mixture of two or more substances. There are no definite proportions by weight for a solution but there is usually a limit to solubility.

Symbol

A symbol is the letter or letters which stand for the name of an element. Symbols are simply a form of shorthand. They are based on the Latin (or internationally accepted) names not on the English names of elements. The brief list below gives some examples of elements and their symbols:

Boron	B
Gold	Au
Hydrogen	H
Lead	Pb
Oxygen	O
Potassium	K
Sodium	Na

It is particularly important that symbols are always written with a capital letter and that when a symbol has two letters that the second letter is small. To write the second letter as a capital may make no sense at all or may mean something quite different. For example Pb means lead but PB implies the existence of a compound consisting of equal parts of phosphorus (Symbol P) and boron.

Formula

A formula is the expression of a compound in symbols. Just as each element has its own symbol each compound has its formula which states of which elements it consists and in what proportions they are combined. The formula for water is H_2O which tells us that hydrogen and oxygen are the two elements in water and that they are combined in the proportion of two atoms of hydrogen to one of oxygen. The number written after and at the base of a symbol tells us the number of atoms of the preceding element which are combined with other elements in the compound. But other larger numbers are also found used before the symbols to which they apply. Perhaps a useful way to think of chemical formula is as a unit of repeat in an overall pattern. For example:

Alumina is Al_2O_3 each molecule consisting therefore of two atoms of aluminium and three of oxygen.

Silica is SiO_2 each molecule consisting therefore of one atom of silicon and two of oxygen.

Water is H_2O each molecule consisting therefore, as mentioned above, of two atoms of hydrogen and one of oxygen.

These then are the individual repeats in alumina, silica and water. In clay these compounds are subject to an overall pattern expressed by $Al_2O_3 2SiO_2 2H_2O$. Thus the compounds which make up clay each of which has its own order are combined in clay in a further order of one molecule of alumina to two of silica and two of water. (This formula of course is the chemical formula and does not show the water physically present in plastic clay.)

Atomic weight

The atomic weight of every element is the weight of one atom of that element in relation to the lightest, hydrogen, which has an atomic weight of 1.

Molecular weight

The molecular weight is the total weight of the atoms making up any molecule.

For example the atomic weight of silicon is 28 and of oxygen 16. The formula for silica is SiO_2. The molecular weight of silica is therefore Si = 28 plus O_2 = 16 × 2 = 32 which is a total of 60.

Acids and bases

There is an important distinction in chemistry between substances that behave as acids and those which behave as bases, all reactions taking place between the two main types. Bases, in glaze especially, are often referred to as fluxes.

The term *alkali* is often confused with *base*. All alkalis are bases but all the bases are not alkalis.

Oxides

Generally speaking the metals form basic oxides and the non-metals the acid oxides. Most of the potter's raw materials consist of oxides which are elements combined with oxygen.

Salts

A salt is a compound of an acid oxide and a basic oxide.

Amphoteric oxides

The main oxide of this type is alumina. Amphoteric oxides are also referred to as 'neutral' or 'intermediate'. They can behave as either acids or bases. They have a very important part to play in the composition of glazes.

GLAZE AND ITS COMPOSITION

The origin of glaze is not known for certain, or whether glass came first though this seems very probable. Through the centuries glazes have been produced and modified by patient empirical experiment and probably sometimes by accident. The recipes of these glazes were often closely guarded and were passed on from generation to generation.

Considerable research has now been made into the nature of glaze. A German chemist, Hermann Seger – who gave his name to Seger cones – was a pioneer in this field. It now appears that though there seems to be an infinite variety of recipes the limits of variation in the composition of glazes are fairly narrow. Though the composition of glazes is not very variable apparently unaccountable differences can be brought about by the use of different raw materials which are chemically, in theory, identical because of minute variations or impurities in those raw materials.

Though it is a combination of an acid oxide and one or more basic oxides glaze is in fact a solution not a salt. Compounds must have fixed proportions of ingredients and the proportions in glazes can be varied. It is now assumed that as a glaze is fired a compound or compounds are formed into which variable amounts of additional material are dissolved. There is a limit to the amount of material which can be dissolved.

The bases or fluxes act as solvents for the silica when the various ingredients of the glaze become chemically active in the heat of the kiln. The neutral, or amphoteric, oxide, alumina serves to give viscosity to the solution. This is not its sole function but without the alumina the glaze would tend to be very fluid and to run. Though glaze is a solid at normal temperatures its nature as a solution at high temperatures enables it to be thought of as a supercooled liquid.

Although the amount of silica which can be dissolved by a given amount of base is variable it is only so within limits. At their simplest these are:
1 unit of base to 2 units of acid (silica) for soft (low fired earthenware) glazes and upwards
1 unit of base to 4 units of acid (silica) for hard glazes (high-fired earthenware and stoneware) and anything in between.

Some high fired glazes have a slightly higher proportion of acid than 4.

For convenience the proportion of base is always kept at 1 and the acid varied in relation to that.

The factors controlling the behaviour of a glaze are:

a the proportion of acid to base
b the kind of base used
c the number of bases used (glaze containing two or more bases being more fusible than glaze containing the same amount of only one base)
d the proportion of alumina to acid (usually $\frac{1}{5}$ to $\frac{1}{10}$)
e the proportion, if it is present, of boric oxide to silica (usually about $\frac{1}{10}$)
f the temperature, duration and atmosphere of firing

The main oxides which take part in the make up of different kinds of glazes are

Basic oxides	*Intermediate oxide*	*Acid oxide*
Lead oxide	Aluminium	Silicon dioxide
Sodium oxide	oxide	(Silica)
Potassium oxide	(Alumina)	
Calcium oxide		
Magnesium oxide		
Zinc oxide		
Barium oxide		

To be able to alter a glaze with confidence it is necessary to know both its formula (its chemical composition) and its recipe (the raw materials used) and in addition to know something of limit formulae.

Glaze formulae and the limit formulae have been arrived at by experiment and collective experience.

The main oxides in the table above which make up the glaze are not all used in their simple forms. Some are corrosive or soluble or poisonous. Some are used in the form of carbonates which makes them easier and safer to handle. Others are specially prepared by fritting. A frit is an incomplete glaze formed by melting a basic oxide or oxides with a certain amount of silica. When cooled this frit is ground to a powder and used as a glaze ingredient. Frits can be made by firing materials in a thick biscuit pot and breaking down and grinding up the resultant glass. In industrial preparation the molten frit is poured into cold water to break it into small pieces and thereby facilitate grinding. This is dangerous unless a fritting kiln is available so individuals who wish to do it will probably have to be content to break up the cooled frit by hand initially. A fairly extensive range of frits, with published formulae, are now commercially available.

Name of glaze	*Firing temperature in ° Centigrade*	*Formula*		
RAW LEAD GLAZES		Bases	Neutral	Acids
Litharge glaze	1060–1080	PbO	$\cdot 3Al_2O_3$	$2\cdot 5SiO_2$
Litharge glaze for raw clay	1100	PbO		
Lead and soda glaze	1060–1100	$\cdot 7PbO \cdot 3Na_2O$	,,	$3\cdot 0SiO_2$
Lead lime and potash glaze	1060	$\cdot 6PbO \cdot 2K_2O \cdot 2CaO$	,,	$2\cdot 5SiO_2$

Name of glaze	*Firing temperature in ° Centigrade*	*Formula*		
FRITTED LEAD GLAZES		Bases	Neutral	Acids
Lead glaze *using sesquisilicate*	1060	PbO	$\cdot 3Al_2O_3$	$2\cdot 5SiO_2$
Lead lime and potash glaze *using monosil: of lead*	1060–1080	$\cdot 6PbO \cdot 2K_2O \cdot 2CaO$	$\cdot 3Al_2O_3$	$2\cdot 5SiO_2$
Lead lime and potash glaze *using sesquisil: of lead*	1060–1080	,, ,,	,,	$2\cdot 5SiO_2$
Lead lime and potash glaze *using bisil: of lead*	1080	,, ,,	,,	$2\cdot 6SiO_2$
Lead and soda glaze *using sesquisil: of lead*	1060	$\cdot 9PbO \cdot 1NaKO$	,,	$2\cdot 5SiO_2$
Lead and soda glaze *using bisil: of lead*	1080	,, ,,	,,	$3\cdot 0SiO_2$
Lead and soda glaze for raw clay	1080	,, ,,	,,	$2\cdot 9SiO_2$

Raw lead glazes

The use of these is not allowed in any schools and is strictly controlled in all contexts.

Fitted lead glazes

The use of these is safer than raw lead glazes but care should be exercised.

With both raw and fritted lead glazes the dangers are minimised if excess glaze is sponged not scraped off, if the glazes are not used by anyone with cuts on their hands and if after use hands and finger nails are cleaned with a nail brush.

RECIPE

Litharge PbO	Lead carbonate $PbCO_3$	Whiting $CaCO_3$	Felspar $K_2A_2O_3 6SiO_2$	China stone $NaKOAl_2O_3$ $6{\cdot}82SiO_2$	China clay $Al_2O_3 2SiO_2$ $2H_2O$	Ball clay	Flint or Quartz SiO_2	Bentonite
54					19		27	
100								
	45			41			14	
	42	5	29		7		17	

Lead monosilicate	Lead sesquisilicate	Lead bisilicate	Whiting	Felspar	China stone	China clay	Ball clay	Flint	Bentonite
	75·5					18·7		5·8	
48·0			6·0	31·0		7·0		8·0	
	52·6		5·6	31·1		7·2		3·3	
		56·7	5·5	30·6		7·1			
	71·4				14·4	13·0		1·0	
		72·7			13·4	12·1		1·6	
		73·9			13·6		12·3		4·0

Name of glaze	*Firing temperature in °Centigrade*	*Formula*		
STONEWARE GLAZES		Bases	Neutral	Acids
Porcelain glaze	1250–1300	$\cdot 08NaKO \cdot 92CaO$	$\cdot 58Al_2O_3$	$3{\cdot}5SiO_2$
Soft stoneware	1200–1250	$\cdot 5K_2O \cdot 5CaO$	$\cdot 6Al_2O_3$	$3{\cdot}7SiO_2$
Medium stoneware	1250	$\cdot 3K_2O \cdot 7CaO$	$\cdot 6Al_2O_3$	$3{\cdot}0SiO_2$
Semi-hard stoneware	1250–1300	$\cdot 5K_2O \cdot 5CaO$	$\cdot 7Al_2O_3$	$3{\cdot}7SiO_2$
Hard stoneware	1300 +	$\cdot 3K_2O \cdot 7CaO$	$\cdot 7Al_2O_3$	$3{\cdot}6SiO_2$
Hard shiny stoneware *for blacks*	1300	$\cdot 5K_2O \cdot 5CaO$	$\cdot 6Al_2O_3$	$4{\cdot}0SiO_2$
Felspathic glaze for raw clay	1250 +	$\cdot 3K_2O \cdot 7CaO$	$\cdot 6Al_2O_3$	$2{\cdot}5SiO_2$
Wood ash glaze	1200–1250			
Wood ash glaze for raw clay	1200–1250			
Wood ash glaze for raw clay	1200–1250			

Name of glaze	*Firing temperature in °Centigrade*	*Formula*		
BORACIC GLAZES		Bases	Neutral	Acids
Lead boracic glaze	1060	$\cdot 7PbO \cdot 3Na_3O$	$\cdot 3Al_2O_3$	$\cdot 3SiO_2 {\cdot} 4B_2O_3$
Leadless boracic glaze	1080	$\cdot 4CaO \cdot 2K_2O \cdot 4Na_2O$	$\cdot 3Al_2O_3$	$1{\cdot}8SiO_2 {\cdot} 8B_2O_3$
Lead boracic glaze *using Fritts of low solubility*	1040–1060			
Leadless boracic glaze *using Fritts*	1190–1240			

Name of glaze	*Firing temperature in °Centigrade*	*Formula*		
MATT GLAZES		Bases	Neutral	Acids
Lime zinc matt	1060–1080	$\cdot 15CaO {\cdot} 35ZnO {\cdot} 5PbO$	$\cdot 25Al_2O_3$	$1{\cdot}5SiO_2$
Alumina matt	1100	$\cdot 35CaO {\cdot} 15K_2O {\cdot} 5PbO$	$\cdot 35Al_2O_3$	$2{\cdot}05SiO_2$
Opaque matt *with additions of 10% tin oxide and 10% Titanium oxide*	1060–1080	$\cdot 9PbO \cdot 1(NaK)O$	$\cdot 1Al_2O_3$	$2{\cdot}4SiO_2$

All excess glaze, lead or leadless, should be sponged not scraped off, the danger from silica dust in the atmosphere.

For testing the safety of fired glazes for domestic use various manufacturers run tests to determine the lead and other metal release factors. Variations of firing and the colouring oxides added to glazes can greatly affect the metal release factor of any given glaze.

Wood ash	*Lead sesquisilicate*	*Lead monosilicate*	*Whiting*	*Felspar*	*China stone*	*China clay*	*Ball clay*	*Flint or Quartz*	*Bentonite*
			23·0		20·0	30·0		27·0	
			13·0	72·0		7·0		8·0	
			20·0	48·0		22·0		10·0	
			12·5	70·0		13·0		4·5	
			18·0	42·0		25·0		15·0	
			12·5	69·0		6·5		12·0	
			22·0	53·0			25·0		4·0
50·0–60·0					40·0–50·0				
50·0							50·0		
1·0				1·0			0·5		

Calcined borax	*Lead sesquisilicate*	*Lead bisilicate*	*Whiting*	*Felspar*	*China stone*	*China clay*	*Ball clay*	*Flint*	*Bentonite*
10·0	56·0				16·0	13·0		5·0	2·0
22·0			11·0	28·0		14·0		23·0	2·0
400·156		25–30			30·0	5·0–10·0			2·0
20·0			5·0	70·0		5·0			2·0

	Lead sesquisilicate	*Lead bisilicate*	*Whiting*	*Felspar*	*China stone*	*China clay*	*Zinc oxide*
		61·6	5·3			22·7	10·3
	47·1		10·0	25·5		16·0	
		80·0			20·0		

Calculating from formula to recipe

Refer to the first glaze of the fritted lead glaze section of the chart on page 122.

The formula for the glaze is

PbO $0{\cdot}3Al_2O_3$ $2{\cdot}5SiO_2$

The problem is to turn the molecular parts of the formula (1, 0·3 and 2·5) into amounts of glaze material. It has been decided to use lead sesquisilicate (formula PbO $1{\cdot}5SiO_2$). The method as shown below is to make a chart having a vertical column for each of the compounds in the formula and using a horizontal line for each of the raw materials. Tables of formulae and molecular weights will be needed. To arrive at the parts by weight of each material the parts needed in the left hand columns are multiplied by the molecular weight of the material.

As the lead sesquisilicate is inserted into the table to supply the lead oxide the first horizontal line can be completed. It must be recognised that as well as supplying the lead oxide required the lead sesquisilicate has also supplied 1·5 of the 2·5 units of the silica needed. China clay is an obvious source for alumina so that is inserted in the second line. The H_2O in the formula will disappear in the firing and is ignored. As well as supplying the necessary 0·3 of alumina the china clay also supplies 0·6 of silica. This 0·6 with the 1·5 from the lead sesquisilicate already gives 2·1 of the necessary 2·5 units of silica. Flint is a source of pure silica so the third line can be completed. As a check the left hand vertical column of the glaze compounds should be added up and compared with the glaze formula and then the column of parts by weight should be totalled so that the glaze recipe can be conveniently expressed as a percentage. In this case the recipe, corrected to one decimal point, is:

lead sesquisilicate	75·5%
china clay	18·7%
flint	5·8%

It should be noted that this fritted glaze recipe comes from the same formula as the first raw lead glaze on the chart on page 122. Exactly the same procedure is followed for calculating more complex recipes involving several bases, the only difference being that more vertical columns are necessary.

Calculating formula to recipe

PbO	Al_2O_3	SiO_2	*Raw Material*	*Formulae of raw material*	*Molecular Weights*		*Molecular Parts*		*Parts by Weight*				*Percentage Recipe (to one decimal place)*
1	—	1·5	Lead sesquisilicate	PbO $1{\cdot}5SiO_2$	313	×	1	=	313	$\frac{313}{414{\cdot}4}$	× 100	=	75·5
—	0·3	0·6	China clay	Al_2O_3 $2SiO_2$ $2H_2O$	258	×	0·3	=	77·4	$\frac{77{\cdot}4}{414{\cdot}4}$	× 100	=	18·7
—	—	0·4	Flint	SiO_2	60	×	0·4	=	24	$\frac{24}{414{\cdot}4}$	× 100	=	5·8
1	0·3	2·5							414·4				100·0

Calculating from recipe to formula

To compare and adjust glazes with certainty it is useful to be able to convert a glaze recipe back to its formula. This, fortunately, is not a difficult procedure.

The stages of the procedure are:

a find the molecular formation of each ingredient in the percentage recipe and its molecular weight and arrange these on a chart as below.

b divide the percentage by the molecular weight

c arrange the ingredients as a formula

d divide the total sum of the base or bases into all the divisions of the formula.

If the lead glaze previously converted from formula to recipe (see chart on page 126) is subjected to these procedures the method should be clear and is shown on the chart below:

To complete the horizontal line for lead sesquisilicate the molecular weight is looked up and divides the percentage to give the molecular parts of each raw material. The various compounds are then inserted into the right hand end of the chart. It must be remembered that each unit of lead sesquisilicate comprises one unit of lead oxide in relation to one and a half units of silica so 0·36 is inserted into the vertical silica column. When all the raw materials have been inserted into the chart the vertical columns are totalled and to express the resultant formula conventionally the total of the basic oxide is divided into the totals of the other materials.

The principle used is applied above to a simple glaze with only one base. The sole difference when several bases are used is that the molecular equivalents of all the bases are added together to reduce the base unit to one and again all the other figures are divided by this.

Calculating recipe to formula

Raw materials in recipe	*Formulae of raw materials*	*Percentage recipe*	*Molecular weight*	*Molecular parts (to two decimal places)*	PbO	Al_2O_3	SiO_2
Lead sesquisilicate	$PbO\ 1{\cdot}5SiO_2$	75·5	÷ 313	= 0·24	0·24	—	0·36
China clay	$Al_2O_32SiO_22H_2O$	18·7	÷ 258	= 0·07 (0·072)*	—	0·07 (0·072)*	0·14
Flint	SiO_2	5·8	÷ 60	= 0·10	—	—	0·10
					0·24	0·07	0·60

PbO	0·24	÷ 0·24	= 1
Al_2O_3	0·07 (0·072)*	÷ 0·24	= 0·3
SiO_2	0·6	÷ 0·24	= 2·5

Bringing basic units to 1

= 1 PbO 0·3 Al_2O_3 2·5SiO_2

*correct to three decimal places

The mixing of glaze

If prepared raw materials are used there are no special procedures for the preparation of materials but if raw materials are being used which have been found or fritted by hand then either pestles and mortars (and a lot of time) are needed or mechanical grinding equipment is needed. Bought prepared glaze materials usually pass through a 200 mesh sieve with little difficulty. Glaze materials prepared by hand, unless a fairly coarse texture can be tolerated, should be ground to pass through at least a 100 mesh sieve.

When mixing a glaze the dry materials are added to water, never the other way round. Materials can be weighed out on any appropriate type of scales. Scales and scale pans should always be kept clean to maintain maximum accuracy. Small amounts of material and colouring oxide and all test material should be weighed on scales which are accurate for very small amounts of material. With recipes expressed in percentages grammes and kilogrammes have long been more favoured as units of measure for potters than pounds and ounces.

When all glaze materials have been weighed out and added to the water surplus water can be poured off (there should always be sufficient water in a container for glaze materials to settle leaving water on top, water can be added as necessary). The glaze is then stirred thoroughly and water can be added to bring the mixture to a thick creamy consistency. Water can be added at this stage as necessary. It is much more convenient to have to add water than to have stirred the glaze with too much water and to be forced to leave it to settle. The glaze can then be sieved. With prepared materials, which have already been sieved, the function of sieving is to remove any coarse material which may have accidentally found its way into the mixture and, importantly, to ensure a fine and even dispersion of the glaze ingredients. Sieving is much easier if glaze is first passed through a coarse sieve, a 60 or an 80 mesh sieve, and is then passed through a finer sieve. With prepared materials a 100 or a 120 mesh is sufficient for colourless glazes but with coloured glazes specks of colour will exist unless the glaze is passed through a 200 mesh sieve (speckled colour may, of course, be wanted). Once a sieve has been used for a coloured glaze it is likely, however carefully it is cleaned, that specks of colour will get into colourless glazes subsequently sieved through it. For this reason where it is possible it is best to have one set of sieves for coloured and another set for colourless glazes and for these to be clearly marked.

Used as they are intended to be, sieve screens, even fine ones, last for a surprisingly long time. If they are misused they will break quickly. Glaze should be brushed through a sieve with a sieve brush, it should never be forced through with a hard rubber kidney or a metal kidney. Soft rubber kidneys used gently will not harm a sieve screen. It should be remembered that a sieve is designed to retain any coarse particles in a mixture – its function is quite different to that of a pestle and mortar which is a fact too often forgotten by many.

The application of glaze

There is no such thing as the right consistency for glaze nor is there a best way of applying it. The right consistency for a glaze depends on the degree of porosity of the biscuit and the thickness which is wanted. The best way of applying glaze depends on the nature of the object being glazed.

When a number of forms have to be glazed at the same time with the same glaze the glaze should be right for the form with the hardest biscuit so that it can be progressively thinned for the softer more porous biscuit.

Before application by any method glaze needs to be thoroughly stirred and may even have to be sieved. Some glaze ingredients tend to sink more quickly than others and if a glaze has settled partial separation may have occurred. The substitution of 1% or 2% of bentonite for the same amount of china clay will greatly improve the suspension of a glaze.

There are three main techniques used in the application of glaze:

Dipping In this process the entire object is immersed in the glaze. Forms with narrow openings are usually glazed inside first by pouring and are then dipped. Forms can be held by hand using as few fingers as possible so that touching up is minimised or, when an entire form is not being glazed, holding the form where there will be no glaze. Alternatively glaze tongs can be used, these allow a whole form to be glazed making only minimal marks. Glaze tongs can be made out of stiff springy wire such as is used in upholstery springs. With dipping as with every other type of glazing it is very important that the entire container of glaze is thoroughly stirred and is of even consistency. Dipping requires larger amounts of glaze than pouring or spraying. Whenever large amounts of glaze are mixed up they should be stirred occasionally even when not needed so that serious settling and hardening does not happen in the bottom of the container.

Pouring The inside of all hollow forms, open or enclosed, is usually glazed before the outside because it is much simpler to glaze the outside of a pot and to be certain of not getting glaze on the inside than vice versa. Pouring the inside is simple: glaze is poured into the form and is poured out, turning the form round so the entire surface is covered. Pouring the outside is usually done with the object being glazed standing on sticks resting on the edge of a bowl which is standing on a banding wheel. The jug is held more or less still and the banding wheel is turned. Bowls, obviously, are glazed upside down. Pots may be where this is possible or the top of a pot may be dipped and then while this glaze is still damp the pot can be stood right way up on the supports and the lower part glazed by pouring. Small pots can be held by hand or with tongs.

Spraying The process of spraying is potentially a danger to health unless it is done in a booth fitted with an extraction fan. Spraying offers a finer control of thickness than either pouring or dipping but some objects of complex form and even simple objects with handles are not easy to spray evenly. Spraying, as well as being a process for applying an even layer of glaze does offer decorative possibilities which have perhaps never been fully exploited.

The painting of glaze is not really a viable process for applying glaze evenly to an entire form. Its use is usually decorative.

Areas of clay which are meant to be unglazed can be resisted with a hot wax and paraffin mixture or with emulsified wax and doing this can save time. Any glaze which has to be removed from feet or other parts of pots should be scraped and sponged off. Scrapings should never be blown off a pot nor should dried glaze ever be brushed off. Dust containing silica is as much a health hazard as are lead compounds and all glaze materials should be handled with care, making the minimum dust possible.

Vapour glazing

It is possible in kilns set aside or constructed for the purpose to glaze clay by inserting material into the kiln which glazes all exposed clay surfaces. This can be done with common salt (sodium chloride), sodium nitrate and with borax and mixtures of these. Using common salt is the commonest practice.

Salt glazing offers the possibility of a rich range of texture and colour. The process is simple. Most clays will salt glaze fairly readily if they can stand temperatures of about 1250°C. Some clays may need silica additions which can be made by adding flint or quartz to the clay. It is the silica in the clay with which the volatilised salt reacts. Salt glazing is done in down draught kilns fired by wood, coal, gas or oil. When the kiln has reached about 1150°C the first salting can be done. Damp salt is thrown into the back of the fireboxes or dropped in through the appropriately placed spy holes. It quickly volatilises. The hydrochloric acid vapour passes through the kiln and the sodium oxide combines with the silica in the clay producing a layer of sodium-aluminium silicate or salt glaze. It is usual to close the damper, if only for a few minutes, immediately after salting to retain the fumes in the kiln. The vapour which passes through the kiln, and can emerge from spy holes and fireboxes while the damper is closed, is highly dangerous and salt kilns should not be in confined spaces. The industrial use of salt glaze is now very strictly controlled because of these dangers. Opinions vary about the best way to carry out salting. Some people advocate frequent small saltings others advocate a few larger saltings. Much depends on the size and type of kiln, the type of ware and the thickness of glaze wanted. It is a usual practice to put test rings in a salt kiln which can be pulled out on a thick wire to see how much salting has taken place. Obviously these test rings should be of the same clay as the work in the kiln. Work in a salt glaze kiln is stood on small pellets of alumina (or alumina and flour mixed 50:50) for which the sodium oxide has no affinity.

Salt glazing can be done quite successfully at temperatures around 1100°C but more usually it is done at about 1250°. The colour range at the higher temperature is richer. Salt glazing affects the inside of pots only very slightly so it is a common practice to glaze the inside of pots. When this is done the temperature reached in the kiln has, of course, to be appropriate. There is no need to biscuit fire pots before salt glazing – the glaze on the inside of the pots can be raw glaze – but the firing cycle has in this case to be appropriately slower than if the pots were biscuited.

Raw glazing

It is usual to biscuit fire pots before glaze is applied to them but this, provided some adjustments are made, is not essential. Raw glazing, the application of glaze to clay at some stage before firing, is possible. Adjustments have to be made to the glaze ingredients to make the glaze layer more plastic so it can shrink with the pot. Ball clay, either completely or in part, replaces china clay. Raw glazing is possible at various stages of dryness but is most usually done in the leather hard stage. Anyone interested in doing raw glazing should experiment both with varying glaze ingredients and applying the glaze at different stages of dryness.

Preparation of ash for glazes

Wood and vegetable matter ash is a variable material. Ash from the same type of tree growing in different soils can be very different and different results can even occur when ash from the same tree made from wood cut at different times of year is used.

Analyses of ash show that ash contains alumina, silica, potash and lime in variable but significant amounts and iron, magnesia and other elements in variable and very much smaller amounts.

Because ash is so variable in composition before contemplating testing it as a glaze ingredient it is essential to have a sufficiently large amount to make the necessary tests and a worthwhile batch.

There are two main possibilities in the preparation of ash:

1 The ash is stirred in water, unburnt material floats to the top and can be removed, the water is poured off and fresh water is added and this again is poured off. The ash is then sieved through progressively finer sieves each time discarding what is left.

2 The ash is dry sieved through progressively finer sieves. This removes unburnt and partially burnt material as this is bound to be relatively large. Each time the material left in the sieve is discarded. (Dry sieving should be carried out only in a spray booth with the extractor fan running or outside.)

The first method washes the soluble material from the ash. This, in removing soluble potash, may well make the ash much harder, that is weaker as a flux, but it may also make it rather less likely to develop the faults associated with a use of soluble fluxes. The second method leaves both soluble flux and the finest partially burnt carbonaceous material.

Unless it is ground up, in one way or another, ash will not go through very fine sieves. It is therefore a common practise to mix the other ingredients together and to sieve these finely and then to add the ash and, to ensure even dispersion of materials, to sieve the mixture through a coarser sieve which the ash will pass through.

Ash glazes have a quality which is unlike any other but because each batch is likely to be different they always require extensive testing if the batch is to have a predictable quality.

A great range of simple ash glaze recipes exist but a sensible initial test to determine the fluxing power of the ash is:

Ash	40%
Felspar	40%
China clay	20%

If this is very fluid the ash is soft (is a strong flux) is at all dry the ash is hard (is a weak flux). Once the power of the ash is known, further tests using felspar, china stone, whiting, china clay, ball clay and flint in simple empirical amounts, as above, can be tried. Ash 50% Ochre 50% is a useful mixture as a thin second layer over an ash glaze and this and smaller amounts of ochre mixed with the glaze ingredients can produce rich and varied colours.

The textural quality of ash glaze is to some extent governed by the amount it is ground up and sieved. The finer the material is, the smoother the actual and visual texture of the glaze. Unsieved ash can be used with clay to give textured surfaces (these certainly could not be called glazes). Unsieved ash (soft) 50% and china clay 50% is a possible starting point for tests of this. Ochre or red clay can be added in increasing amounts to replace the china clay and darken the glaze.

Tests of coloured glazes

In theory because the metal oxides which act as colouring agents in glazes take part in the glaze reaction (often as fluxes) a glaze recipe should be adjusted to compensate for this. In practice this is rarely done and the glaze recipe ingredients are left adding up to 100% and the colouring ingredients are additional to this. Coloured glaze recipes therefore may often total over 100%.

Whenever glaze tests are being made accuracy, especially in the weighing of the colour ingredient, is essential. A mistake in a glaze test of 100 grammes can make a great difference when a batch of five or ten kilogrammes is being mixed.

Initial testing of oxides and colours should be done at 1%, 4%, 7% and 10% to determine the relative strength of the colour or oxide. Amounts over 10% can produce interesting results but do tend to affect the behaviour of the glaze, sometimes quite considerably.

Blending of colourless and coloured glazes by mixing known proportions of fluid glazes of the same consistency to effect a dilution of colour, or by mixing two coloured glazes to effect a mixing of colour, is a quick way of making tests but tests done by this method are of dubious accuracy and before a batch is mixed the results of the fluid blending should be checked in a weighed test. If weighed tests are allowed to dry out after use the dry glaze can be used to make accurate blended tests by weighing.

It is a wise precaution to test every freshly mixed batch of glaze before it is used extensively, simply to check that no mistake was made in the mixing.

THE COLOURING PIGMENTS

The colouring pigments used in pottery are all derived from metals: some come from common metals such as iron and copper, some from precious metals such as gold and some from unfamiliar ones such as selenium. The oxides of other metals, such as zinc, have a marked effect on the colours that are formed in their presence. The actual colour produced by any pigment is always very importantly affected by the context in which it is used.

The actual colour produced by any pigment is controlled by four main factors:

a the temperature of firing – some pigments become unstable and volatilise at temperatures well within the normal range of firing temperature.

b the atmosphere of firing – colours produced in oxidisation and reduction atmospheres can be fundamentally different.

c the other materials, both the colour producing and colour modifying ones, with which the pigment is in contact.

d the amount of the pigment used – different concentrations of pigment can produce different colours as well as different tones of one colour.

The metallic pigments are, of course, the same as those which colour rocks and stones in nature.

The list of pigments which follows includes the main colouring pigments and describes the colours which they produce. Materials which are difficult to obtain, such as uranium oxide, or are dangerous, such as antimony oxide or are very rare have been omitted. Where a raw pigment is difficult to obtain or is dangerous it is usually possible to buy prepared colour or glaze which contains it.

Antimoniate of lead

Antimoniate of lead is a pigment of medium strength and gives yellow in the presence of lead. As a source of yellow, because of its need for lead, it is no use in stoneware where the lead in the pigment volatises and all that is left is antimony oxide which gives a milky grey. In earthenware the yellow is much stronger when the pigment is in or over a lead rather than a leadless glaze. When used as a painting pigment a tendency towards dryness can be minimised and the strength of colour improved if the antimoniate of lead is mixed with an equal part of a lead frit.

Chromium oxide

Chromium oxide is an excellent example of an oxide which produces fundamentally different colours in different contexts. It is a very refractory pigment and is not readily soluble in glazes. Chrome oxide is a deep green powder in its raw state and it gives in different contexts a wide range of colours. About 0·5% to 1% in an earthenware glaze with a high lead content the chrome will dissolve and produce, over a white body or slip, a translucent yellow. In the same context larger amounts will not dissolve and the colour becomes progressively greener. In low fired (900°C to 1000°C) glazes with a high lead content 0·5% of chrome will produce a translucent yellow, about 1·5% an orange and 2·5% an opaque red. Painted over a tin glaze chrome becomes unstable and in volatilising produces a pink flush known as 'chrome-tin pink'. This reaction is remarkably strong and chrome and tin should always be very well separated in a firing. The reaction forms the basis of a range of prepared colours made by calcining tin oxide with chrome oxide (or lead chromate or potassium bichromate) with borax, flint and whiting. The colours which this reaction can produce range from pink to crimson – red and pink to lilac. The prepared colours can be bought both as underglaze colours and as glaze/body stains.

Cobalt oxide

Cobalt oxide is a very strong blue pigment. It is a strong flux. As a pigment it is stable at all pottery temperatures.

Used as a painting pigment cobalt oxide can be ground with china stone in various ratios to dilute it. One part of cobalt oxide to ten parts of china stone still gives a strong blue. In some contexts appropriate materials other than china stone can be used.

In glazes 0·1% is not an unreasonable starting point for tests. So little cobalt is needed that its fluxing power may not be obvious but very little blue glazed pottery is produced industrially because the fluxing power of cobalt is so great that glaze surfaces tend to be unacceptably soft and scratchable.

Though a strong pigment cobalt is affected by its context. It tends to be brighter in leadless glazes than in lead glazes. Zinc oxide and whiting both help to make the colour more brilliant.

In glazes containing magnesium cobalt loses its blueness and gives mauves and mauve pinks.

Very, very minute amounts of cobalt have occasionally been used either in the body or the glaze to 'whiten' slightly cream firing bodies.

Copper oxide

Copper oxide is a versatile pigment. Two sources are commonly used: cupric oxide, which is a black colour, and copper carbonate, which is green. In reducing conditions cuprous oxide is formed. Copper has a fluxing effect on glazes but this is not as powerful as cobalt. It is slightly volatile in oxidising firings and more so in reduced firings.

In earthenware lead glazes copper gives greens in amounts up to about 3%. The same amount in lead glazes rich in lime gives brighter green. In alkaline glaze 2% to 3% gives green turquoise. In soda glazes which are free of alumina about 2% gives a real blue/green turquoise. Excessive amounts of copper will produce crystalline blacks in any glaze.

In stoneware glazes copper gives greens in oxidising conditions and a range of pink to red in reduction. In reducing conditions copper is volatile and will 'flash' both from pot to pot in a kiln and through the walls from inside to outside a pot.

Iron oxide

Iron oxide is the most all pervasive pigment in nature. Few ceramic materials are entirely free of it. It is a useful pigment both in producing a range of colours and in modifying other colouring pigments. As well as using the oxide itself (which occurs in several different forms) various earths rich in iron, such as yellow ochre, may be used.

Iron has a marked fluxing effect in clay but in glazes it does not behave as a strong flux. It is fairly readily soluble in lead glazes more so in stoneware glazes but is only slightly soluble in leadless earthenware glazes.

In lead earthenware glazes iron produces a range of colour from pale amber yellow to dark terracotta brown. 6% gives a rich amber. After about 6% the iron tends not to dissolve readily and 10% tends to be an opaque brown.

In oxidised stoneware iron gives a range of colour from tan to deep brown.

In reduced stoneware colours range from pale blue greens (from 0·5% to 1·5%) of the celadon range to deeper greens at 8% to rich browns and black at 10% and slightly over. The palest celadons can only be achieved on porcelains and very white firing stonewares or bodies covered with white slip. Iron impurities in body or glaze are often sufficient to give a pale celadon.

Oxides of manganese

The most usual form used is manganese dioxide. Manganese is a powerful flux.

In earthenware lead glazes manganese produces browns (2% to 5%). In soda earthenware glazes 2% to 3% gives a purple. In other earthenware alkaline glazes it gives a purple brown and at stoneware temperatures gives browns with only a hint of purple.

Nickel oxide

Nickel oxide is stable at all normal pottery temperatures. Nickel is rather unpredictable and is the source of some glaze faults, for this reason it has been somewhat avoided industrially. It can, in different contexts, give a range of colour which includes browns, greens, grey-greens and grey-blues.

Tin oxide

Tin oxide is a white powder which is almost totally insoluble in glazes. It is very refractory and is stable at all pottery temperatures. Incorporated into a glaze mixture tin oxide remains in suspension and makes the glaze white and opaque. Its most usual use is in glazes in amounts rarely over 10% but it can also be painted over coloured glazes as a white pigment. If dryness of surface is to be avoided in this latter context it should be mixed with an equal amount of an appropriate frit or glaze material.

All the oxides listed above can be mixed with each other, though the resultant colours are not always predictable. Before tests of combinations are made it is important to understand that the oxides differ very considerably in their relative strengths. This will be best understood if varying amounts of each oxide alone (say 1%; 4%; 7% and 10%) are tested in a glaze. It will be found that 1% cobalt oxide is roughly the same tone as 7% of iron oxide.

Though the list of oxides above is small the range of colour that can be produced by mixing and by application in differing contexts is very great. This range can be further extended by using prepared colours of various types. The range available is briefly described below.

Prepared underglaze colours and glaze and body stains

These are prepared by calcining the oxides and combinations of oxides with various other ceramic materials. The colours are totally different to those which can be achieved by using uncalcined mixtures. Some colours go through several calcining processes. The colours are more stable and predictable than those from oxides and oxide mixtures but just as with oxides they are not in themselves absolute colours and their actual colour always depends on the context in which they are used. Like oxides they can be mixed with each other (they can also be mixed with oxides) and like oxides the results of mixing are not always predictable.

Underglaze colours

Though called underglaze colours these can equally be used for painting onto unfired glaze. Most manufacturers supply two types: those which are stable to any earthenware or stoneware temperature; those which are only stable at earthenware temperatures.

Glaze and body stains

These are modifications to pigments produced very similarly to underglaze colours to make them more suitable for additions to glaze, slip and clay. They can be used in varying strengths. Manufacturers usually suggest maximum amounts. The colours can be mixed but, as usual, the results are not always predictable. Manufacturers stipulate which colours are suitable for any pottery temperature and which are stable only at earthenware and in addition stipulate which colours are suitable for glazes and bodies and which are suitable for glazes only. The precise colour is of course always dependent on the quantity used, the temperature of firing and the body and glaze used.

FIRING

The firing of pottery involves the controlled application of heat to a sufficient degree and for a sufficient length of time for certain chemical and physical changes to occur. The process is not simply a temperature process it is also a time and temperature process.

This is a cold factual description of the process of firing. In fact the firing of kilns is surrounded by a certain mystique. Even the most precise and efficient people experience a certain excitement when a kiln is opened – nothing, it seems, is totally predictable. This lack of predictability is unfortunate but it is real and it is due to the extent of human fallibility and to the relative complexity of the whole pottery process. The reason is not that kilns, as is sometimes supposed, have a life and mind of their own.

Firing is the culminating process in which the craftsmanship and experience which have gone into making an object at various different stages are put to the test. The control of the firing itself is also a part of that test. The test is a rigorous one.

It is unfortunate that the mystique of firing is such that beginners can sometimes expect their work to shatter inexplicably into fragments when it is fired. The idea that the firing can make everything wonderful is the other side of the beginner's misapprehension. If everything about pottery making and firing were absolutely controllable the things which emerged from any kiln would be totally predictable. Most people will accept that some things about ceramics are not entirely controllable and where this is the case (and it is certainly not the case in every aspect) each person must decide on acceptable limits of variation. Two examples of aspects which are not precisely controllable are the textures which can develop from double glazing with earthenware glaze – the degree of textural mottling depends on the relative thickness of the two glazes and even with great experience this is not precisely controllable – and the colours and textures which are produced in glazes in stoneware reduction firing – even if glaze application through long experience is of known thickness the actual duration and strength of reduction can greatly affect the fired result and even with vast experience it is virtually impossible to precisely repeat the schedule of a reduction firing.

This discussion of control and precision may seem strange in the context of a discussion of firing but it is important that firing is understood to be an important part of the whole pottery process. The aura of mystique which so often surrounds it does little to encourage an understanding of it which is so essential if the whole process is to be understood and used.

Disasters in firing will always occur and have always occurred. It is important that disasters and happy and unhappy firing accidents are studied for, as much as the things which occur predictably, they can lead to a greater understanding of processes and materials.

206 A Sung dynasty waster. A celadon bowl has fallen onto a bottle during the firing and stuck to it. What is interesting is the way the bowl has distorted over the shoulder and neck of the bottle almost like soft, plastic clay. This shows the extent of the softening which happens during vitrification of stoneware.

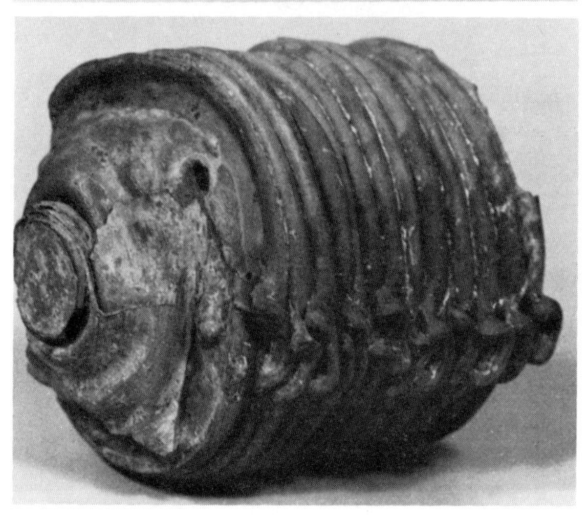

207
208

A Roman waster of a stack of something over twelve bowls. This was either an untested choice of material or the result of overfiring. The clay has bloated badly and begun to fuse so the entire stack of bowls is stuck together. This is a good example of the fusing of secondary clay. Within a remarkably small temperature span fusible secondary clay can change from being an acceptably hard biscuit to being a useless brittle half-boiled mass.

Types of kiln

Electric kilns are the most controllable of kilns. For clean low temperature and earthenware firing they cannot probably be challenged. Models are now available which fire up to 1300°C but their biggest drawback is that unlike other stoneware kilns they are suitable only for oxidised stoneware. The fumes of combustion, if material is inserted into the kiln to promote reduction, do seriously affect the metal of the heating elements and shorten its life. Thermostatic control devices can be fitted to electric kilns to control speed of temperature rise and time at maximum temperature which in fact make the firing entirely automatic.

The vast majority of kilns have heating elements made of an appropriate grade of Kanthal wire. Kanthal Al is used for work at 1300°C. This is remarkably long lasting and reliable but is not meant to stand reduction fumes. In fact quite a few potters use electric kilns for producing reduced stoneware and minimise the wear on elements by alternating oxidisation and reduction firings. Nevertheless the life of kiln elements is considerably shortened by this. A few electric kilns are now produced which do permit reduction. These use special elements made of silicon carbide which is exceptionally durable and is unaffected by reduction. It is also exceptionally expensive. Reduction is effected either by fitting such kilns with small gas burners to burn up the oxygen or by introducing combustible material into the kiln.

Gas kilns Two basic types exist: the open type where the flame and fumes of combustion pass through the chamber and therefore are in direct contact with the ware and the enclosed muffle type where the flames heat an enclosed box and are not in contact with the ware.

The open type is good for any type of stoneware. Reduction is induced by control of the damper which partially shuts off the chimney and delays the passage of fumes through the kiln and control of the air intakes which can be partially closed to starve the flame of oxygen. This type is not good for earthenware especially for lead glazes which tend to blister if in direct contact with flames.

The muffle type of kiln is very adaptable indeed and can be used for any type of firing as the flames do not come into contact with the ware. Reduction is induced either by means of a purge burner, a small burner linked to the inside of the muffle, or by introducing combustible material into the muffle. Gas kilns are available to burn main gas or bottled gas. All gas kilns require a substantial flue.

Oil kilns There are two different types, the drip feed type and the atomised feed type. It would be very rare to find an oil-fired kiln with a muffle, all tend to be of the open type with the flames in direct contact with the ware.

In the drip feed type oil is dripped onto either an inclined metal channel or a series of inclined metal plates which it runs down and burns as it falls over the end or in the later stages of firing ignites as it hits the hot metal. Water is sometimes dripped as a separate drip alongside the oil to supply oxygen for combustion. The process of drip feeding by itself is not very efficient. Temperatures of 1300°C can fairly easily be reached but only with extravagant use of fuel. The type can be made more efficient if air is blown through the burners. Drip feed kilns will work with paraffin or fuel oil or mixtures of these with discarded sump oil.

The atomised feed type is far more efficient in its use of fuel. Several systems are available but the basic principle is the same. A compressor supplies compressed air through pipework to a burner at the firebox mouth. Gravity fed oil is supplied to the same burner and is atomised into a spray which burns in the firebox. These burners are both efficient and reliable and maintenance is very simple. There is one drawback to the system which is that the heat output though very finely controllable when the kiln is hot is very difficult to control when it is on very low. For this reason initial heating of the kiln is often done with a bottled gas burner. Systems of compressors and burners do tend to be expensive to buy.

Solid fuel kilns Wood, coal and coke are all possible solid fuels. Two drawbacks exist: firstly the use of solid fuels is now controlled by local bye laws concerning smokeless zones, which effectively limits their use to the country and secondly solid fuel kilns require far more attention than any other type of kiln. A third drawback with wood is that unless a suitable cheap supply is available locally it can be very expensive.

Solid fuel kilns are more complex structures than oil or gas kilns. Oil and gas both have fireboxes but because of the nature of the fuel and the complete absence of ash these can be very compact. Wood, coal and coke all require substantial fireboxes to retain the burning and unburnt fuel and hearths to collect the ash as it falls through the firebars.

Two types of solid fuel kiln exist: updraught and downdraught. In updraught kilns the heat enters at the bottom of the chamber and passes through the wares to a chimney on top. With downdraught kilns the heat enters the kiln and partly tends to rise and partly is forced to rise over a wall of refractory material and leaves the kiln at the bottom from where it is drawn through to a chimney. The downdraught type is the more flexible and the more efficient. It is rare to find solid fuel kilns with a muffle. For this reason as the flames are in direct contact with the ware they are mostly built as stoneware kilns. Control of atmosphere is effected by adjustment of the damper usually inserted between the chamber and the chimney and by restriction of the air entering the firebox.

Wood was the fuel used by the Chinese and, probably partly because small amounts of ash are deposited on ware in the kiln, wood does impart a particular quality to stoneware glazes.

Use of saggars Any kiln of the open type – gas, oil or solid fuel – can be used to fire work which may be affected by direct contact with flames if the ware is placed in saggars, which are simply large vertical sided boxes into which glazed pots can be placed to protect them from the direct action of flames during a firing. All lead glazed earthenware was fired in saggars before the advent of electric kilns. Now that there is such a range of possible fuels and kilns to suit different requirements the use of saggars is rare.

The process of firing Whatever type of kiln is being used what happens during the first firing of clay is much the same.

The ware is put into the kiln in as dry a state as possible. Even in this state it is likely to contain 5% or more of water. The heat must be applied evenly and slowly to drive off this water. If the kiln reaches 100°C before this water has been driven off the pot can shatter into pieces as the boiling water changes to steam. The clay will continue to break up until all the water has escaped as steam. What is really happening is that the surface area of the clay is being increased until the water can readily escape. Providing pots are as dry as possible when they are put in the kiln and the kiln is heated very slowly to start with this need never happen. The evidence of this sort of explosion is quite unlike any other disaster and is quite unmistakable, the clay affected will be found in lots and lots of small fragments. Fine plastic clays are more susceptible to this than coarser clays.

Once this point is passed and all the free water in the clay has been driven off the firing can be speeded up, but temperature rise is fast if it exceeds much above 130°C per hour. By 700°C all organic matter will have burned away and the clay will have given up its chemically combined water. There are several stages at which these complex changes in structure occur and if the speed of firing is too fast fine cracks can occur in the clay. From 700°C new silicates form and fill up the pores in the clay and contraction occurs. The firing should proceed to whatever is the desired biscuit temperature and then the kiln should be allowed to cool. As fired clay cools there are two points at which changes occur in the crystal structure, one is between 575°C and 550°C and the other is at 225°C. Cooling should be even and not too fast at these stages.

Packing kilns

Packing any type of kiln is a job which should be done in as organised and clean a manner as possible. Ware which is waiting to be fired is almost always in one sense or another fragile – either it is unfired and easily chipped or broken or it is biscuit fired and covered with a fragile layer of glaze or it is glazed and has areas of fragile overglaze colour – so packing should be planned so that the ware has the minimum amount of handling necessary.

There are a few basic rules to observe in the packing of all kilns which concern the use of shelves and props and their placing in the kiln.

The rules are:

a three columns of support not four are used. These are at the corners of the longer side and in the middle of the opposite side.

b the columns of support which continue from shelf to shelf must be directly above the columns of the shelf below.

c before placing in the kiln every shelf should be held at one corner and tapped with a metal tool such as a cold chisel. If it rings the shelf is sound, if it is cracked it will sound cracked and should be broken in half.

d shelf props should be tapped and otherwise examined for cracks – this is especially true of the taller type propping systems.

e any glaze specks sticking to a shelf or prop from the previous firing should be chipped off.

In addition it is advisable to try to keep shelves with a top surface and an underneath. This does mean they may warp more quickly than if they are turned but it does eliminate the possibility of bat wash specks or flakes dropping onto glazed ware. The top surface of shelves and the meeting surfaces of props should be painted with bat wash before they are ever used. This helps to minimise the sticking of specks of glaze. This bat wash layer should be repaired whenever glaze has to be chipped off it.

If they are carefully looked after the life of shelves and props can be very long. It should be remembered that uneven cooling is much more harmful to shelves than sudden cooling. Exposing the edges of shelves in a tightly packed kiln by opening the door and leaving it open is a frequent cause of cracked shelves.

Shelves and props are most usually made of a very refractory alumina based body. Silicon carbide shelves and props are also available. These are much stronger and more durable and very much more expensive.

Various systems of props are available.

Kiln shelves should be brushed top and bottom before each firing to remove any loose particles. Between firing shelves should be stacked preferably on wooden racks to minimise the danger of mechanical damage. They should be stacked on edge topside touching topside and underside touching underside so that flakes of bat wash do not get onto the underneath of shelves.

209

Packing a biscuit kiln In a biscuit kiln pots can touch each other. Forms of the same size like saucers can stand one inside the other. Cups and bowls can be fired in stacks resting edge to edge and foot to foot.

Ventilation bricks and spy holes should remain open until well after all the free water in the clay has been driven off.

Packing an earthenware glaze firing No part of any glazed object can touch anything in a kiln without sticking to it. When earthenware is glazed all over it is supported on stilts or saddles. Stilts have one or three sharp points and come in different sizes. Those with single points are placed around a form. Those with three points usually support a small single form alone. Saddles have a sharp edged triangular cross section and are usually used radially to support a form on its footring. Both saddles and stilts stick to the fired piece and need breaking off. The resultant scar is touched to smooth it with a grindstone. Scars are minimised if the object is moved slightly on its supports before firing thereby removing excess glaze. Earthenware with the glaze cleaned off its foot can rest directly on a kiln shelf.

No less than stoneware earthenware glaze firings should be soaked, that is held at or very near the top temperature, to give the glaze time to mature properly.

Packing a stoneware glaze firing No glaze must touch any part of any shelf or prop or kiln structure or other pot. Glaze must be cleaned off the bottoms or feet of stoneware pots very, very thoroughly as the vitrification which occurs in stoneware clays makes them more prone to sticking than earthenware. The smallest amounts of glaze not cleaned off can stick a pot to a shelf very securely. A good unbroken layer of bat wash is absolutely essential with stoneware. Some movement and distortion of forms is not uncommon at stoneware temperatures so while it is safe with earthenware glaze firings to place objects very close it is wiser with stoneware to allow 13 mm between all objects.

Packing an overglaze kiln for enamel or lustre As the ware is not heated to a point where the glaze softens no stilts are needed. But objects cannot be stacked as the enamel and lustre do flux. The major point to watch in stacking is scrupulous care not to damage the colours. In firing the major point to watch is that all ventilation bricks and spy holes are left open until the smell of evaporating medium has disappeared.

When packing any kiln other than an electric kiln or a kiln with a muffle allowance must be made for the circulation and flow of heat and gases through the kiln. Packing without due consideration for the flow of gases can make a perfectly good kiln quite useless. The problem does not exist with muffle kilns and electric kilns but with these every effort should be made to distribute the work as evenly as possible in the kiln.

Firings after the biscuit firing are not attended by the same risk of shattering explosion and may be taken more quickly but the kiln should be well ventilated till the water absorbed from the application of glaze has been forced off. When vitrified ware is being refired it should be fired more slowly than glazed biscuit as too sudden a temperature rise can crack it.

All unfired glaze and oxide tends to come off onto the hands and leave finger marks on the next object touched. In any type of packing every effort should be made to keep the hands as clean as possible otherwise finger marks will certainly be left.

Temperature measurement

Firing most kilns is fairly straightforward. Electric kilns are simply turned on and turned up; gas and oil kilns are regulated by controlling the amount and ratios of the fuel and air available for combustion; control of solid fuel kilns is more complex but the principles involved are the same as with oil and gas even though the mechanics are less obvious.

Providing a kiln is efficient and is capable of reaching temperature the problem is not so much one of controlling the heat but it is one of measuring the temperature and thereby knowing what needs to be done. Various means of temperature measurement are available.

Pyrometers Pyrometers consist of a temperature indicating gauge and a temperature measuring thermocouple. Thermocouples consist of a twin metal (usually platinum/rhodium) rod encased in a refractory tube. The uneven expansion of the metal creates a tension which transfers current down a flexible cable to the temperature indicating gauge. Pyrometers are very useful as when readings are regularly recorded they can show the rate of temperature rise and cooling within a kiln. To get an idea of the heat differences in top and bottom of a kiln a thermocouple can be removed from and inserted into different holes in a kiln.

Temperature control equipment can be linked to pyrometers on electric and gas kilns.

Pyrometric cones

Cones are small cast forms of various ceramic materials designed to begin to melt and therefore collapse at a precise temperature. Even when a pyrometer is used it is advisable to use cones as well, as a double check. Cones should be placed exactly

210 Cones are set into clay. If the kiln is to fire fast the clay should be pierced all over with a matchstick to facilitate drying and minimise the danger of the clay exploding and the cones falling over.

211 Two fired cones, perfectly bent.

behind spyholes and at least 50 mm inside the kiln. If they are placed too close to the spyhole they will tend to be cooler than the kiln because of draught. If cones alone are being used it is best with electric kilns to have two cones one of which is one below the temperature required and one of which is the actual temperature. Soaking can be started when the first cone bends. Knowing how much to turn down a particular kiln comes with experience and the amount depends on the condition of the elements and the amount of work in the kiln as well as other factors but on no account must the correct cone be allowed to bend more than half down which is the point at which the actual desired temperature has been reached. With gas, oil and solid fuel kilns most people prefer to have several cones warning before the maximum temperature is reached. For reduction stoneware firings of say 1300°C it is usual to include a cone of about 1050°C to mark the point when reduction should begin.

Until any kiln is thoroughly known it is advisable to put a few cones into different parts of the kiln to record any cool or hot spots which may exist. This sort of checking should be done over several firings so that it is the behaviour of the kiln which is recorded not simply the unevenness which may result from a single packing.

Two sizes of cones exist: standard which are approximately 64 mm tall and miniature which are 29 mm. The standard have the advantage of being easier to see and the disadvantage of taking up more space.

Many people advocate the use of one cone over the desired temperature as a check that temperature is not being exceeded.

Bars Bars are quite simply an alternative to cones. Unlike cones they are placed horizontally both ends being supported and they collapse in the middle when temperature is reached. They are smaller than standard cones but more or less the same size as miniature cones. They take up less space than standard cones but are less easy to see at very high temperatures.

Atmosphere and firing: oxidisation and reduction

In electric kilns and muffle kilns no combustion is taking place inside the kiln and oxygen is freely available to any materials which tend to combine with it. The firing is therefore oxidised. To create reduction in these kilns (ignoring for a moment the damage which can occur to kiln elements) all the free oxygen in the kiln has to be burnt up and then the available oxygen has to be removed from those oxides where this is possible. To do this combustible material has to be introduced into the kiln (mothballs, which burn very well but may give off obnoxious vapours, can be rolled down a tube through the spyhole, or thin sticks of wood can be inserted through the spyhole). This material will quickly use the oxygen in the kiln and then seek out other available oxygen. This it can find in the oxides of iron and, where it is present, copper. As oxygen will be finding its way into the kiln all the time this combustion has to continue so the atmosphere is constantly starved of oxygen and the oxides affected are reduced. Just as they can be reduced the oxides can reoxidise. Not all the oxygen is removed from iron and copper oxides by reduction: iron reduces from ferric oxide, Fe_2O_3, to ferrous oxide FeO; copper reduces from cupric oxide, CuO, to cuprous oxide, Cu_2O.

In kilns where the flames and fumes of combustion are in direct contact with the ware reduction can be effected more simply by limiting the air available for combustion. This is done in one of three ways or a combination of them all. The air supply can be cut right down so insufficient oxygen is entering the kiln to completely burn the available fuel which therefore seeks out other sources of oxygen. The damper can be closed or partially closed to limit the flow of gases through the kiln and thereby limit the oxygen entering the kiln. A brick or bricks can be removed from the bottom of the chimney which allows air to enter and go up the chimney which creates a back pressure similar to inserting the damper limiting the flow of air into the kiln. The visible signs of reduction in any open kiln are that flames emerge through spyholes and cracks in the brickwork and, usually, that black smoke emerges from the chimney. Flames should just emerge from holes in the kiln they should not rush out strongly if they do this latter reduction is probably too strong.

The reduction of stoneware should begin before the glazes soften at about 1050°C so that the body is well reduced before the glaze softens. If the glaze softens first reduction of the body will be inhibited by the fluid glaze and will be patchy and incomplete. Reduction should continue, usually with occasional periods of oxidisation to clear smokiness, until temperature is reached and soaking completed. Usually the firing is finished with a ten minute period of oxidisation to clear any carbon trapped in the glazes. This, after a thorough reduction, is not long enough to permit either glaze or body to reoxidise. Because reduction is not a process which can be finely controlled results, however experienced the person controlling the firing may be, tend to differ slightly from firing to firing as the actual degree of reduction does finely affect the textures and colours achieved.

Section Four Some decoration processes

INTRODUCTION

Apart from its form, which can range from the austerely simple to the elaborately complex, pottery, from its earliest beginnings, has provided a ground for graphic treatment of great variety. Some of the processes by which pottery can be decorated have very close parallels in other contexts. Other processes are unique to ceramics. The sections which follow describe some of the processes by which pottery can be decorated and are illustrated with traditional examples of the uses of those processes. There is on the whole a rightness about traditional uses of technique mainly perhaps because in times when fashion changed more slowly, and life was slower, and there was less demand for change, it was difficult to sustain the contrived or inappropriate use of technique. The danger then was more one of deadness through over abundant skill and familiarity – through slickness – rather than deadness through contrivance. It is true that most processes and materials used in decoration lead naturally to the making of particular qualities. This becomes evident both by experiment with the processes and materials and by a study of traditional uses of those processes and materials. The danger of course is that of eclecticism. It is perfectly possible to study traditional uses of processes and materials and to learn something of their potential qualities without thoughtlessly copying the content of those uses as well. Unfortunately there have been periods when processes and content have been thoughtlessly and lifelessly copied. In reaction to this there have also been times when too narrow a knowledge of processes or materials has led to a contrived and inappropriate use of the processes and materials known.

Anyone who has an interest in decorating should endeavour to experience as many as possible of the various processes and materials that are available. The range available and the related range of qualities is great. To decorate with choice and freedom in pottery demands a knowledge of this wide range.

Some questions applicable to decoration

There are no rules except the rules which each individual formulates for himself according to his own criteria. Rather than rules or principles there are aspects of decoration to question. These questions are really only an aid to criticism and self-criticism. The first question 'Do I like this?' usually has a quick answer. Whether that answer is positive or negative there are other questions which can and should be asked and which serve perhaps as a framework within which to consider a particular example. The questions are not fixed definite ones but can be made about the following aspects of decoration.

Scale

Scale is the size relationship between the form and its decoration and also sometimes between the elements of the decoration. When it is being decorated, with the possible exception of modelled decoration, the form to which the decoration is being applied has an established size. The idea of the decoration can be applied in a variety of scales. No single scale is the only possible scale in any instance but consideration of right scale is always important.

Balance

Balance is the distribution of colours, tones, lines, areas over a surface. Balance can be a static, quiet quality or can be dynamic. It can be achieved as much by complete asymmetry as by symmetry.

Contrast

Contrast of line, shape, tone or colour can be strong or subtle. Contrast is simply difference and exists inevitably in all decoration. The type and degree of contrast always need to be considered.

Repetition

Repetition is an interesting aspect. Perhaps it is often thought of too narrowly and consciously as being the repetition of a made unit of design but it does exist of a much more basic level in repetition of colour, tonality and line width, all of which may often be accepted without thought once chosen but can be varied by simple means.

Repetition within one object is a related problem to the repetition of objects such as plates on a table or wall tiles. In the latter case the repetition is usually the identical repetition of a whole unit. In the former case repetition can be considered more broadly. One aspect of a unit can be repeated while another is varied, for example, the width of a line may be repeated but its length or its colour may be varied or the shape of an area may be repeated and its size or its colour may be varied.

Content

The content of decoration is its starting point. Originality is not a quality that is consciously achieved, it is one which occurs.

Striving towards it is probably responsible for more contrivance and dullness than anything else. One's starting point can be humourous or mathematical or representational or abstract or purely experimental with materials (on a conscious level). Sincerity perhaps is the most important aspect of content.

The content of decoration may occur spontaneously or it may be preconceived and carefully planned out. The first step in physically carrying out a decoration is the choice of materials which determine colour, tone and texture. The tools used determine to some extent the quality of line and mark which will occur but this is also controlled by the materials used and the state of those materials. Consideration of scale, balance, contrast, repetition and variety can occur both during work and when it is complete. A final point worth mentioning is that it is sometimes instructive to ask how much one is imposing on materials and how much the materials are dominating. With all the different qualities available it is important to realise that some materials and processes allow precision and some do not. Whatever its content and however well considered are the various aspects of decoration there needs to be a sympathy and an understanding of the processes and materials being used for a decoration to have that quality which gives it life.

AGATE WARE

Agate ware can be produced by mixing together two or more clays of different colours. It can be made both by mixing together clays which are naturally different in colour and starting with a white clay and making other colours by adding oxides or body stains. If clay is too overloaded with colouring it can start to bubble badly. With some oxides this can begin to occur at about 10% of oxide to dry clay. But obviously colour tests should always be made.

To actually make an agate body the different clays can be mixed in various ways. However the clay is mixed the work is usually produced in moulds by cutting sheets from the block of agate clay. With experiment and experience the general nature of the agate markings can be controlled quite well. When mixing the coloured clays together every effort should be made to ensure they are of the same consistency. If possible it is a good idea to leave newly mixed agate wrapped in polythene for a few days for it to become even in consistency. Agate sheets can be quite freely modelled in a type of slab building. Agate may also be thrown but this destroys the characteristic markings produced when it is moulded and produces a steady spiral marking. The markings of thrown agate are only crisply revealed if the whole pot surface is turned.

212 A Staffordshire cat about 1745 *Victoria and Albert Museum*

213 A Chinese cup of the Tang Dynasty *British Museum*

INLAY

214 Fragment of a mediaeval inlaid tile found at Chertsey *Victoria and Albert Museum*

Inlay is produced by filling impressions or scratched drawn lines made in soft clay with either slip or plastic clay of a different colour. If slip is used it is applied immediately after the drawing or impressions have been made. Slip is more appropriate when the marks are fairly fine. With large deep marks slip tends to shrink and crack away from the body clay and it is anyway not easy to fill deep large indentations with slip. When plastic clay is used this is pressed into the sunken marks as soon as there is no danger of the marks being distorted. Slip is sometimes sparingly used to ensure a good join between the clays. With both slip and plastic clay the surface of the object is scraped clean at a firm leather hard stage to reveal the sharp inlay.

A very rare type of pottery known as Henry II ware and produced in France in the reign of Henry II is decorated with very fine inlay but on the whole the most common use of inlay has been on tiles. Tiles of course are easier to scrape down to reveal the inlaid design.

215 Mediaeval tile found at Chertsey *British Museum*

SLIP TRAILING

216 A detail of a dish decorated by Thomas Toft (Staffordshire, second half of the seventeenth century).

There are two variations of slip trailing: it can be done straight onto a plastic clay ground and it can be done onto a wet slip-covered ground. In the former case the slip tends to stand up in relief somewhat, in the latter it can sink into the slip ground to form a smooth surface. The basic units of trailing are a line and a dot. Free areas can be made by pouring slip into areas sponged clean of the ground slip and by spreading this slip to fill the cleaned area. Slip trailing, it should be remembered, uses a fluid medium for drawing. This is not to say that precision and control should or can not be aimed at but it does mean that either the confidence of experience should be considerable or that an idea should be fairly clear.

Trailing can be done onto flat sheets of clay and these can subsequently be moulded over a hump mould. It is common practice both with trailing done onto sheets of clay and with trailing on shallow bowls and dishes to jolt the pot or the board with the clay on it down onto a table to flatten the slight relief of the slip. This is better done when all trailing is completed otherwise the first trailed lines will be spread much farther than the last.

Ideally trailing is done with the nozzle fractionally above the clay surface. If the nozzle is allowed to move over very soft clay it may produce a hollow with ridges each side which can detract from the trailed line.

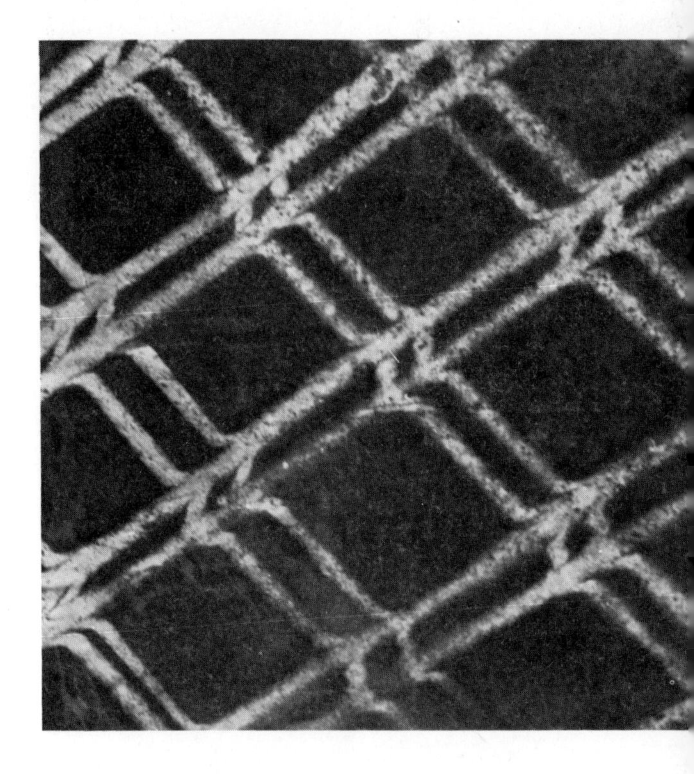

217 A detail of a geometrically trailed dish. Staffordshire, eighteenth century. Slip trailing is done by applying slip to the surface of a pot from a 'trailer' fitted with a nozzle to limit the flow of slip. The rubber bulb type of slip trailer permits instant control of the flow of slip and the size of nozzle determines the amount of slip available and therefore the width of line.

FEATHERING

Feathering of slip is simply a subsequent treatment of trailed lines. Any fine-pointed tool – a brush, a feather, a needle even – is drawn across the wet slip surface. The tool will move the line slightly or considerably depending on the delicacy of the stroke and the nature of the tool. Historically the technique was generally used to create a grid pattern from lines trailed parallel to each other. But it can be used, and has been, less mechanically to add finer lines to a slip trailed design.

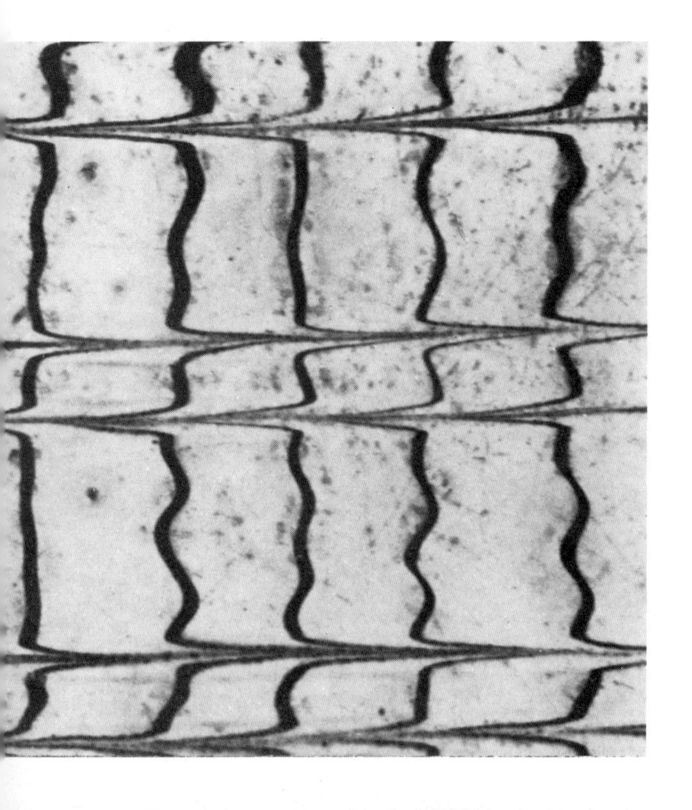

218

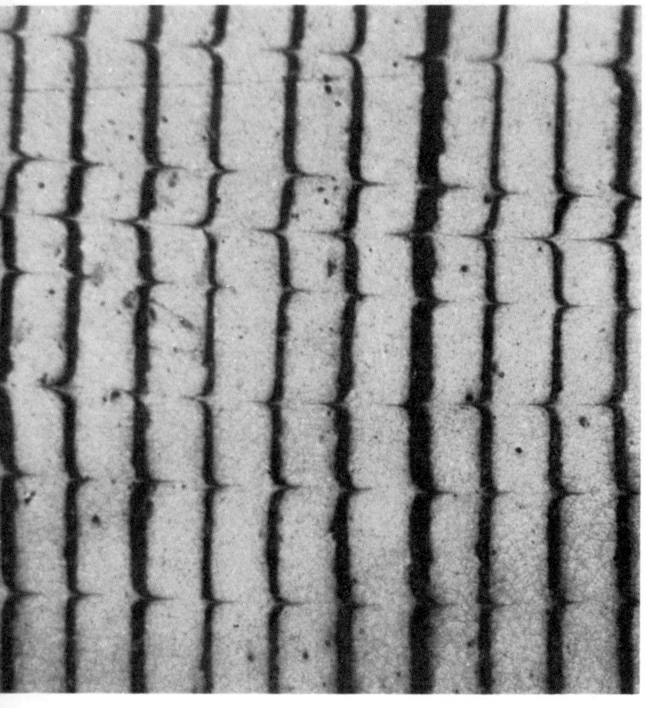

219

Details of feathered trailing on eighteenth century dishes.

MARBLING

220 Detail of marbling on an eighteenth century dish. *Victoria and Albert Museum*

A clear distinction should be made between marbling and agate. Marbling is a surface treatment using fluid slips of different colours. Agate is a clay body composed of different coloured clays.

Marbling is, like agate, a rather random process but, like agate, with experiment and experience a degree of control can be achieved.

Marbling is done very simply by covering a clay object with thick slip and then trailing or pouring or even splashing another slip into it and then tilting, turning, tapping, shaking or even spinning the clay object to move and mix the different slips. This moving of the slip should always result in some slip being poured off the object which reduces the slip layer to a reasonable thickness. It is not possible to produce richly swirling marbling if the ground layer of slip is of normal thinness.

SPRIGGING

221 German salt-glazed Bellarmine, seventeenth century.

Sprigging is the making of small moulded decorative forms and the application of these to clay objects. Sprigging is either applied directly by 'rolling' the slipped back of the sprig, still in its mould, directly onto the pot or by removing the sprig and applying it separately, which is usually done by pushing a knife flat onto the reverse of the sprig to lift it from the mould and move it to the pot and position it when it can be fixed in position with a little slip and by carefully pushing into the hollows with a wooden tool.

Sprigging can be done in the same clay as the body of a pot and left to work simply as relief or it may be done with a clay of contrasting colour.

Moulds for sprigging can be cast from modelled clay or carved wood or other material but one of the possibilities of the process will not be fully realised unless some sprigs are carved into plaster. Carving a sprig in reverse does permit the use of very fine scratched lines which in the cast clay sprig are reversed into fine lines of relief.

222 English earthenware mug with sprigged date.

MODELLED DECORATION

Technically there is little to say about modelled decoration except that the clay which is added to the pot or form should be as similar in consistency as possible, that it is usually done as early as possible in the hardening and drying cycle of the pot (in fact as soon as it can be done without the risk of distorting the form) and that slip or water, as appropriate, are used to join the modelled clay onto the form.

The modelling may simply be a surface decoration or it may take the form of knobs, handles or feet. Modelling may of course be done in clay of a different colour to that of the pot.

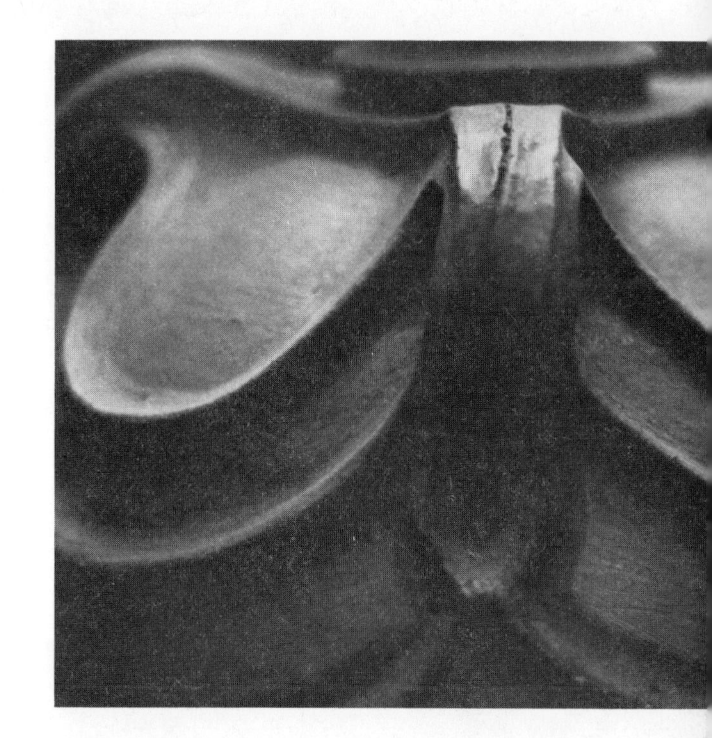

223

224

Bold relief decoration on African pots *British Museum*

IMPRESSED DECORATION

Impressed decoration can either be done into the body clay of an object or it can be done into softer clay applied to the surface of an object. There are two possible variations of impression making: impressions, both small and simple or larger and complex, can be impressed into the clay as single units (and, if so intended, can be repeated) or they can, from stamps of cylindrical form, be rolled onto the clay to make a band of impressions. This latter technique is called rouletting. A roulette may be round and thin like a coin when it will produce a fairly thin line of impressions or it may be round and much thicker, like a cotton reel when it will produce a broader band of impressions. Roulettes are sometimes used to texture pots at the turning stage and can be applied, in this case, while the pot is on a wheel. Stamps and roulettes can be made of any hard material such as fired clay, plaster, wood and metal.

225 Detail of impressed decoration on a large pot from Camirus, Rhodes, seventh century BC *British Museum*

GROUND LAYING

Ground laying is the application of a flat, even colour ground either onto entire surfaces or small reserved areas. The surfaces being ground laid must be thoroughly cleaned of dust and grease from fingerprints. The ground laying oil is then painted on fairly thinly and as evenly as possible with a good quality soft broad brush and is left to develop the right degree of stickiness. The time this takes depends on the heating and ventilation of the room. It is vital that ground laying is done in an atmosphere which is as dust free as possible. When its consistency is just right the painted layer of oil is patted out with a dabber made of cotton wool wrapped in a small piece of fine real silk. This patting out, or bossing, operation spreads the basically even painted layer until it is even in detail that is until all the brush strokes and streaks are removed. When the layer is quite even and still sticky powdered colour is then applied with a pad of cotton wool. The cotton wool itself should never touch the surface so it should be well loaded with colour. The powdered colour sticks to the oil surface and surplus loose colour can be removed by dusting with a cotton wool pad.

Ground laying is a skilled, and, in the industrial context, expensive process. When skilfully done it can produce areas of even flat colour more successfully perhaps than any other ceramic process. The success of the operation depends to a very great degree on the evenness with which the oil is brushed on and the evenness of the bossing operation.

In a day or two the ground laying oil dries hard and the surface can be carefully touched. It is possible to scratch through the hardened oil and colour to make designs. Equally, if this was the intention, even before the ground laying oil is applied areas can be resisted and when this has been done the resist is washed off at this stage when the colour and oil have hardened. In the past vermilion water colour mixed with water with a little syrup dissolved in it was the material used for resist. This was painted on and allowed to dry and then the ground-laying oil was brushed onto the ware and over the resist as necessary. When the oil and colour had hardened the resist was removed by washing in cold water leaving the unresisted areas clearly defined. The hardened oil is unaffected by the water. This method still holds good but paint technology is changed and changing and it is wise to test that the particular brand of colour chosen does in fact wash off with cold water when dry.

Ground laying oil can be mixed and consists of gum mastic, pure turpentine, linseed oil and litharge (lead oxide). Its preparation is elaborate and a little tricky. It is easier and probably wiser to buy it ready prepared.

SGRAFFITO AND INCISING

Sgraffito and *incising* are both used to cover a range of closely related processes. More strictly a distinction can be drawn if 'sgraffito' is applied to marks which remove one material and reveal another and if 'incising' is applied only to marks which are made directly into clay.

Sgraffito

Sgraffito is capable of very varied treatment and may be done with a variety of materials. It may be a purely linear treatment or whole areas of material can be removed. Sgraffito may be done through slip or oxide back to a clay body, it may be done through a layer of glaze back to clay, or it may be done through a second layer of glaze or a layer of overglaze colour back to a fired glaze and there are other variations as well.

At whatever stage it is done and with whatever materials it will be found that the control and the quality of mark made depend on the materials being used, the state of those materials and the nature of the tools being used. Some materials in certain states allow a considerable degree of precision. The same materials in other states and other materials may not.

With slip on clay a very wide range of qualities are possible. The slip can be removed as soon as it is applied – though strictly this is closer to combing than sgraffito – it can be removed when it is just touch dry, when it is leather hard and when the slip and clay body are bone dry. Work at the different stages will have very different qualities and possibilities.

226 Sgraffito through white slip to a red clay body, eighteenth century, Staffordshire.

Victoria and Albert Museum

227 Sgraffito through white slip to a red clay body. One of a set of tiles from Tring in Hertfordshire, fourteenth century. *British Museum*

Incising

Perhaps it may be a little difficult to strictly delineate between 'incising' and 'carving'. Carving is comparatively rare with clay but it might be said that illustration 229 is an example of carved relief rather than incised decoration. The distinction is an academic one and the two processes, if they have to be thought of as separate, are in practice very similar.

Exactly as with sgraffito through slip into clay the qualities evident in the process of incising vary considerably depending on the stage at which it is done. Precise fine lines can be incised into bone dry fine-textured clay but if the clay contains grog or sand the line will have a much more jagged quality. A fine line drawn into soft clay will leave a burr standing up on each side of the line. A fairly firm leather hard condition does allow marks to be made with certainty using a range of fine and broad cutting tools. Experiment should be made with a range of tools, a range of conditions of clay and a range of types of clay.

Incised marks can be left to read simply as relief on unglazed objects. They can be filled with slip to make inlay or can be treated in a number of ways with oxide. One treatment that is common and has been used at various times by various cultures is, with light firing clay, to glaze the incised pot with a single pale glaze. When this is done the glaze picks up the relief, however slight, running off high points and gathering in low points and incised lines. This very simple direct treatment is full of possibilities.

228 A tablet of cuneiform writing sharply incised into leather hard clay, *British Museum*. Though communicative rather than decorative in intent the visual effect is very rich.

229 A Sung Dynasty stoneware plate with a green celadon glaze.

PRINTED DECORATION

In about 1760 a process was invented to transfer a printed design onto pottery. Though some hand processes still exist in the industry, printing, very soon after its first application to ceramics, quickly became the major decoration process and technical advances are constantly being made. Engraving, lithography and screen process printing are all applicable and each has different possibilities. For some processes manually applied transfers are necessary, for others the ware itself is directly and automatically printed with a flexible gelatine pad. Screen process printing can be done directly onto certain shapes.

The major possibility of printing processes is obviously in its large scale industrial application. The aspect of printing of most use to schools or individuals is, in that it can be well done without very costly and sophisticated equipment, screen process printing.

230 A tile with a printed engraved decoration by Sadler and Green about 1770, Liverpool
Victoria and Albert Museum

LUSTRES, GOLD AND PLATINUM

The lustres used in the decoration of Islamic and Hispano-Moresque wares depended for their quality on a reducing firing. This technique was revived in the nineteenth century by William de Morgan and more recently experiments have continued. The industry has developed lustres which do not require reduced firing.

Salts or carbonates of copper, silver and gold are the bases of the traditional lustres. These are mixed with ochre and applied to the glazed ware in a thin film. The lustre is developed by reducing when the kiln reaches temperature and maintaining a reducing atmosphere while cooling takes place.

Industrially prepared lustres contain local reducing agents and so require no special firing procedure. They are applied in a thin film by brushing.

Gold and platinum are respectively the bases of gilding and silvering painted on over the glaze. Silver itself is not used because of its tendency to oxidise and blacken.

Prepared lustres and gold and platinum should be used and fired with careful adherence to the maker's instructions. With some aspects of pottery accidents can sometimes be happy accidents but this is in no way true of these materials which are prepared for precise use in precise conditions. If they are not used and fired as intended they rarely work at all.

PAINTING

More than any other, painting is a process open to very wide application. Slip, oxide, enamel, glaze, lustre and the precious metals can all be painted and there is a vast range of prepared under and overglaze colours of various types. Many of these materials can be used in more than one context.

The three sections which follow should only be seen as a brief introduction. They are by no means exhaustive.

Slip painting

Painted slip being a much thinner layer than poured slip tends to behave very differently to it. Slip painted onto a clay body and fired once can be decidedly non-opaque – the body can show through distinctly and brush strokes almost always show. When glazed slip painting, if too thin, can disappear almost completely. Learning to judge and control the thickness of painted slip is an essential prerequisite for successful use of the process.

The tendency for painted slip to be translucent can be reduced if the oxide content of slip for painting is much higher than would be used for pouring. This is certainly what was the practice when slip was widely used as a medium for painted decoration. Soft thick brushes that can be well filled should be used for slip painting and the slip should be thick enough in consistency to stand up in slight relief. If historical examples of slip painting are studied it will be found that like slip trailing the units of decoration are the line (sometimes, admittedly, a broad calligraphic stroke) and the dot. Painted areas are not found and if attempts are made to make them it will be found that they are either messily uneven or that the areas have to be built up layer upon layer to be even.

No painted slip will be absolutely even in tone and colour and the quality of slip painting depends a great deal, whatever may be the stylist conventions current, on the directness and freshness of the application of the brush strokes – this is just as true of the highly controlled planned decoration of Geometric Greek pottery as it is of freely calligraphic painting on Tzu Chou pottery (see illustrations 233 and 235).

The process known as *paté-sur-paté* is a very logical extension of the process of slip painting. The process was used a great deal by a Frenchman called Solon who worked initially at Sèvres and from 1870 until 1904 at Mintons. The technique, simply, is to build up a decoration in slight relief by painting many layers of porcelaneous slip over a coloured body. The slip varies in translucency where it is varying thinnesses and is opaque where it is thick.

231 A painted fragment from Persia, 4000 BC
British Museum

232 A pot from Cyprus, about 2000 BC

233 An early Geometric period Greek bowl, ninth century BC

234 A glazed bowl from Samarkand, ninth century AD *British Museum*

235 Tzu' Chou ware, Chinese, Sung Dynasty *Victoria and Albert Museum*

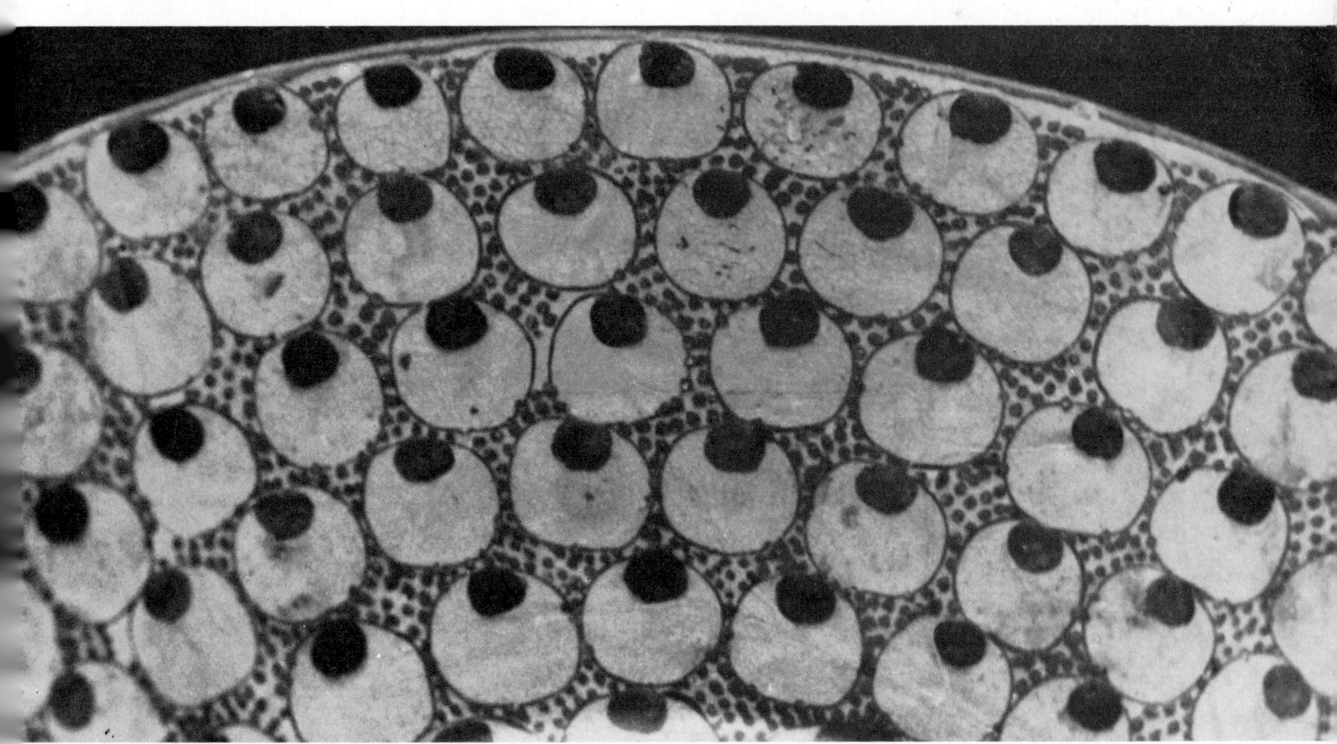

Underglaze painting

When painting is done onto biscuit the colour should be mixed with underglaze painting medium but whenever possible the painting should be done before firing. It is worthwhile to experiment with painting on surfaces of different drynesses. For painting on unfired clay colours are mixed with water only. The process offers very considerable control of thickness – the water carried colour can be evenly spread on damp clay. Differing tones of one colour can easily be built up with dilution by water alone.

To be at all even colours need to be well ground. This can be done with a glass muller on a glass slab or with a palette knife on a glazed tile but unless it is done very thoroughly the colour is likely to be spotty.

Prepared underglaze colours and the metal oxides, the latter with suitable additions, can both be used and can be mixed with each other for underglaze painting. Mixing does not always give the results which one might expect.

Underglaze colours and mixtures should be well tested. It is useless to work from a manufacturer's colour chart. The colours and mixtures should be tested on any clays they might be used on and should be glazed with lead and leadless (and, if appropriate, one or two stoneware) glazes. The colours can vary greatly in differing contexts. Any test should show a grading from thick to thin.

Spiral banding and concentric bands and lines can be applied to round forms on a banding wheel.

The more recent manifestations of underglaze painting have unfortunately been rather dead repetitive work at the cheaper end of the industry but the process, especially when done on unfired clay, has very varied and interesting possibilities which have not been investigated for a very long time.

236 Detail from a dish from Isnik, Turkey about 1560–1580 *British Museum*. Underglaze painted on a white slip ground.

237 Detail of an eighteenth century Chinese porcelain plate painted in underglaze blue the decoration copying a Dutch tin-glazed original. *Victoria and Albert Museum*

On-glaze painting

This was the technique of the Italian majolica painters and of the Delft ware potters of Holland. Some on-glaze painting has been done on stoneware and porcelain but, in general, on-glaze painting is the process of painting onto a white tin glaze with the metal oxides and oxide mixtures, though, of course, there are other possibilities.

The best condition in which to paint the glaze is when it is just touch dry but still distinctly damp. For this reason the biscuit should be high-fired but certainly not vitrified and just before glazing should be quickly dampened. The glaze itself should be thicker than normal, about the consistency of distemper. Glaze goes on to dampened pots more smoothly and evenly than on to very porous pots. Piccolopasso in his book, *The Three Books of the Potter's Art* written 1556–1559, describing the whole process of majolica production likens the thickness of glaze to thick glove leather and this seems a very apt description. A glaze applied as above will dry very slowly so no problems of dryness will be encountered during painting – if a glaze surface becomes too dry before or during painting the wet, colour-filled brush can tend to roll or peel glaze off or make it bubble up. But if preparation for it and glaze application itself are right no problems should be encountered during painting.

The oxides used for painting on to tin glaze are antimoniate of lead and iron, cobalt, manganese and copper oxides. Nickel oxide can also be used. All the oxides can be mixed and tin oxide can be used as a part of a mixture. As well as being mixed the oxides can be superimposed. No medium of any kind is needed. The colours are simply prepared by grinding thoroughly in water on a glass slab or a tile. Antimoniate of lead is best used mixed with an equal part of a lead frit. Cobalt and copper, which can both tend to be a little strong, can be considerably diluted with china stone.

Painting onto the unfired glaze surface 238 A Delft ware tile from Holland, mid-eighteenth century, painted in cobalt on a tin glaze *Victoria and Albert Museum.*

Tin glazes have very little tendency to run. The most common fault is crawling. The beginnings of crawling can usually be seen with tin glaze before the glaze is fired. If a network of fine cracks covers the unfired surface of the glaze then the best answer is to scrape the glaze off and begin again for, unless they are exceedingly fine, these cracks nearly always develop into serious crawling.

As well as the usual oxides prepared on-glaze colours are also available and these exist in considerable variety.

239 Detail of an eighteenth century Chinese 'Famille verte' plate *Victoria and Albert Museum*

240 Detail of flower painting in enamel colour on English eighteenth century porcelain *Victoria and Albert Museum*

Painting onto a fired glaze surface This strictly is usually called overglaze rather than on-glaze painting. It is done with enamels, which are prepared colours made by fusing oxides and oxide mixtures with soft frits of borax and lead, and also, as mentioned elsewhere, with lustres and precious metals.

Enamel painting can be done on the surface of any type of glazed ware but in that enamel colours offer a wider, brighter range of colour than that available at higher temperatures and with other materials the process is usually done on white glaze (or clear glaze on white clay) so that the full potential of the colour can be used. One of the rather beautiful qualities of enamel colours is their translucency and this too is obviously best developed on a white ground.

Enamel colours need to be just as carefully fired as glazes. Underfired by a few degrees they can tend to be sticky looking and rather obviously superficial. Well fired they soften and blend more with the glaze on which they are fired.

The colours are mixed with a painting medium and should be applied with soft brushes.

Appendixes

TABLE OF ELEMENTS COMMONLY FOUND IN CERAMIC MATERIALS, THEIR SYMBOLS AND THEIR ATOMIC WEIGHTS

Element	*Symbol*	*Atomic weight*
Aluminium	Al	26·98
Antimony	Sb	121·75
Arsenic	As	74·92
Barium	Ba	137·34
Boron	B	10·81
Cadmium	Cd	112·40
Calcium	Ca	40·08
Carbon	C	12·01
Chlorine	Cl	35·45
Chromium	Cr	52·00
Cobalt	Co	58·93
Copper	Cu	63·55
Fluorine	Fl	19·00
Gold	Au	196·97
Hydrogen	H	1·00797
Iron	Fe	55·85
Lead	Pb	207·19
Lithium	Li	6·94
Magnesium	Mg	24·31
Manganese	Mn	54·94
Nickel	Ni	58·71
Nitrogen	N	14·01
Oxygen	O	16·00
Platinum	Pt	195·09
Potassium	K	39·10
Selenium	Se	78·96
Silicon	Si	28·09
Silver	Ag	107·87
Sodium	Na	22·99
Sulphur	S	32·06
Tin	Sn	118·69
Titanium	Ti	47·90
Uranium	U	238·03
Vanadium	V	50·94
Zinc	Zn	65·37
Zirconium	Zr	91·22

Not all these elements play an active part in the changes which occur during firing but in calculations it is important to know atomic weights even though the element may volatilise during the firing.

CONES

Various types of cones are available. The two commonest are Standard Seger cones and American Orton cones temperature equivalents for which are given below. Both these types are based on a temperature rise of 150°C an hour. (If the temperature rise is slower the cone will bend slightly earlier than the stated temperature).

Because the numbering systems of cones are so similar it is important that it is quite clear which type of cone is being used otherwise confusion and mistakes in firing can occur.

Standard Seger Cones temperature equivalents

Cone No.	*Temp. in °C*	*Cone No.*	*Temp. in °C*
019	685	01a	1105
018	705	1a	1125
017	730	2a	1150
016	755	3a	1170
015a	780	4a	1195
09a	935	5a	1215
08a	955	6a	1240
07a	970	7	1260
06a	990	8	1280
05a	1000	9	1300
04a	1025	10	1320
03a	1055	11	1340
02a	1085		

American Orton Cones temperature equivalents

Cone No.	*Temp. in °C*	*Cone No.*	*Temp in °C*
022	600	05	1046
021	614	04	1060
020	635	03	1101
019	683	02	1120
018	717	01	1137
017	747	1	1154
016	792	2	1162
015	804	3	1168
014	838	4	1186
013	852	5	1196
012	884	6	1222
011	894	7	1240
010	894	8	1263
09	923	9	1280
08	955	10	1305
07	984	11	1315
06	999	12	1326

GLOSSARY OF SOME TERMS USED IN POTTERY

This list mainly, but not exclusively, includes terms not used in this book. See the index for references to terms used in this book.

Air bubbles Small pockets of air trapped in a clay body. These can make working difficult but it is a complete myth that air causes clay to explode during firing. When clay with air bubbles does explode what occurs is that the water evaporates from all surfaces and in the enclosed air pockets cannot escape. If the firing is fast this water, which condenses in the pockets, can cause explosions (see page 138). But if the firing is slow there is no problem – it is possible to safely fire completely enclosed hollow forms.

Air bubbles can also form in glaze if insufficient time is allowed for the glaze to mature and for gases to escape.

Armenian bole An iron earth which can be used as a painting material. It is found on Persian and Turkish pottery.

Basalt ware Pottery made black by the addition of oxides and/or calcined colours. Basalt ware was used extensively for objects in classical revival styles. There is no natural black basalt clay.

Bat The term may be used to refer to both refractory kiln shelves and discs of plaster, asbestos, wood or fired clay used for throwing on.

Bat wash A slip of alumina and water painted on to kiln shelves and props to minimise adhesion and to facilitate removal of glaze specks.

Beehive kiln See *Bottle kiln.*

Bellarmines See illustration on page 150. Salt glazed bottles originally made in Germany. The bottles are ornamented with a face mask originally representing Cardinal Bellarmine. Bellarmines are a common type of vessel and form part of an extensive tradition of bottle forms decorated with faces.

Biscuit ware or bisque Pottery which has been fired once and has no glaze.

Blisters Bubbles formed in the body of pottery and projecting from it. Blisters are formed by gases which are unable to escape because of too fast a firing. Reduction atmospheres can aggravate blistering. The term is also, but less commonly, applied to bubbling in glaze.

Block mould See *Master mould.*

Blunger A machine for mixing pottery bodies and other materials in a fluid state. Blungers are containers in which paddles revolve. They are filled through the top and the fluid mixture can be drained off through taps in the bottom. Hand blungers are portable mixers which can be used in appropriate containers.

Body As used in the text the term refers to the clay mixture of which any pottery is made – as, for example: porcelain body; coarse body; dark body; terracotta body, etc, etc. The term is also used to refer to the main form of a pot – other related terms are obviously: neck; foot; shoulder.

Bone china An English type of china or porcelain which is something of a hybrid between true hard porcelain and, the now obsolete, soft paste porcelain. It contains bone ash (calcined animal bones) and is very white and translucent. It has a high biscuit firing and a lower temperature glaze firing.

Bottle kiln Sometimes also called beehive kiln. A traditional type of large kiln circular in plan, tapering, bottle shaped, towards the top and fired with coal or coke. As a production kiln these have now been totally superceded by tunnel kilns.

Bung A vertical stack of loaded kiln shelves (or saggars).

Calcine To reduce to a powder or to a friable state by an appropriate heat. The actual temperature depends on the material being calcined.

Calcareous clay Clay containing lime, often called a *marl.* If present in clay lime must be finely subdivided.

Celadon The name given to a range of green stoneware and porcelain glaze colours derived from iron. The colours were first evolved in the Far East.

Chattering Also, called *juddering*. A surface irregularity caused by vibration which can occur during turning. It is caused by any one of various factors including blunt turning tools, coarsely grogged clay, and holding turning tools loosely.

Clamming The sealing up of kiln doors with a mixture of wet clay and sand or grog.

Collaring A process used in throwing to narrow a pot or part of a pot. Both hands encircle the form and move steadily upwards pushing inwards.

Combined water The water which is chemically combined with clay. Once driven off by the heat of firing it cannot be replaced.

Combing The working of wet slip into patterns using a comb made of card or wood or leather. A similar process to feathering but it can be done through slip to a body of contrasting tone or colour as well as across the surface of different coloured slips.

Continuous kiln A kiln which the ware is moved through allowing continuous firing.

Crackle A network of fine cracks in a glaze due to a greater shrinkage in the body than the glaze. The term is generally applied to the intentional use of this phenomenon for decorative purposes.

Craze A network of fine cracks in a glaze as described under *Crackle*. The term generally implies the unintended occurrence of cracks in a glaze. Crackle and crazing should not occur on vessels used for food or drink as the fine cracks can retain material. When crazing occurs on a porous body it is very unhygenic and in severe cases the body itself can become badly stained.

Creamware A cream-coloured earthenware developed in the mid eighteenth century and popular until the beginning of the nineteenth century when whiter bodies became more favoured.

Deflocculants Substances that interfere with the natural cohesion of the particles of plastic clay and make it fluid. Soda ash and sodium silicate are deflocculants and introduced in the proportion of approximately $\frac{1}{2}$% into soft plastic clay will reduce it to a thick runny slip.

Delft ware Loosely used to describe pottery glazed with an opaque white tin glaze and usually painted. The name originated from the town of Delft in Holland where such pottery was produced.

Devitrification The formation of crystals in a glaze. This can be caused by very slow cooling as well as by the presence in glaze of certain substances which tend to crystallise out of the mixture. Zinc and titanium both promote crystallisation.

Diatomaceous earth (Kieselguhr) A form of silica which consists of the skeletons of microscopic marine animals – diatoms. It is extremely light and makes excellent insulating material for kilns both in powder form and made into bricks.

Dod-box See *Wad-box* and *Extrusion*.

Down-draught kiln A kiln in which heat and flames either enter the kiln at the top, or are deflected towards the top, and are drawn downwards and out through flues at the base of the back wall or in the floor of the kiln.

Drawing a kiln Unpacking it after firing.

Dunting The cracking of fired pots during cooling caused by uneven or too rapid cooling. There are two critical points in a cooling cycle which must not be passed too quickly one is between 575°C and 550°C and the other is 225°C. At these points silica in the body undergoes certain changes which are accompanied by a change of volume. If cooling is fast or uneven at these points dunting will occur.

Efflorescence White scumming which sometimes occurs on the surface of terracottas (and other biscuit ware). It is caused by soluble salts present in the clay and can be overcome by the addition of about 2% of barium carbonate to the clay which neutralises these salts.

Engobe Loosely the term is sometimes applied to all slips. More specifically it is used for mixtures of clay and frit (and colour too sometimes) which are painted in a slip state onto clay. Engobes can be more readily built up to opaque thickness than slips.

Encaustic tiles A nineteenth century term for inlaid tiles.

Extrusion The forcing of clay through a die forming it into lengths of specific cross section. Extrusions can be solid as with extruded handles or hollow as with drainage pipes. Small extrusions are generally done in a manual wad-box larger ones in a mechanical extruder rather like a pugmill.

Faience The French term for earthenware. Not a word of specific meaning. The word comes originally from the Italian town of Faenza which exported large quantities of tin glazed ware to France.

Fat clays General term for clays with plastic qualities. Clays lacking such qualities are referred to as *lean* clays.

Fettling Cleaning away of mould seams from slip cast ware. Sometimes also used loosely for any general cleaning up of pots.

Filter press Substantial machine for squeezing water out of slip to produce plastic clay.

Flat ware Industrial term for plates, shallow dishes, saucers, trays, etc. Cups, bowls, jugs, teapots, etc. are termed *hollow* ware.

Flaking or scaling Can occur to slips during drying or firing and is caused by a difference in shrinkage. It can also occur to glaze prior to firing. In both these cases the slip or glaze materials need changing to give more or less shrinkage as appropriate. Scaling of fired glaze can also happen at the edges of pots. To correct this adjustments have to be made to the body, usually to its silica content.

Gilding The application of gold by various processes to pottery.

Glost firing Glaze firing.

Green ware Dry unfired ware.

Grès The French term for stoneware.

Grès de Flandres Salt glazed ware from the Low Countries.

Hard paste (*Paté dure* in French) A term used for the true porcelain which originated in China. Soft paste (*Paté tendre* in French) is the term used for European attempts to copy this by introducing frits into the body.

Hare's fur The name given to a stoneware iron glaze which has flowed slightly giving a soft fur like linear texture. *Tea dust* and *oil spot* are very similar glazes which have a different textual quality. All three were originally descriptions of glaze quality in Chinese stoneware.

Hollow ware See *Flat ware.*

Intermittent kiln Any kiln of any type in which the ware has to be packed, fired, cooled, and unpacked. The term has only been in use since the advent of continuously firing tunnel kilns and in fact refers to all kilns other than these.

Ironstone china A non translucent but very hard dense body in vogue in the nineteenth century. Mason's Ironstone China is the best known but there were many varieties. Much experiment was done with hard white earthenware bodies at the beginning of the nineteenth century and these are often difficult to categorise.

Juddering See *Chattering.*

Lamellar Describes the microscopic structure of clay – that of thin flat scales.

Lawns The woven screens of sieves made of phosphor bronze wire in varying degrees of fineness. The grading of lawns into 60, 100, 200, etc. indicate the number of wires per linear inch.

Lean clays See *Fat* clays.

Leather Chamois leather often used for finishing thrown edges and for fettling.

Leather hard Clay that has, through drying, lost its plasticity but is not yet dry and is still impressionable with a finger nail but not with a finger print.

Lugs Side projections on pots functioning as handles.

Luting The fixing together of two clay surfaces with slip.

Majolica A term used for Italian tinglazed ware and, loosely, for the technique of painting onto tin glazed ware.

Marl Clay containing lime.

Master mould Block mould; the mould from which working moulds can be cast.

Mishima The name given to a type of fine inlay in black and white found on some Korean pots.

Moving hearth kiln The term is most usually applied to intermittent trolley kilns (those where the trolley is packed, moved into the kiln, fired, cooled, moved out of the kiln and unpacked). But obviously tunnel kilns also are, strictly, moving hearth kilns.

Muffle A fireclay chamber or box that protects pottery from direct contact with flames and kiln gases.

Opening materials Non-plastic materials such as sand or grog which can be added to a body to open it up that is to facilitate drying by giving it a coarser texture. Doing this reduces shrinkage and may also increase refractoriness.

Open firing Firing in which the pottery is exposed to kiln gases and flames, unprotected by a muffle box.

Oil spot See *Hare's Fur*.

Parian body A porcelainous body, used unglazed, popular in the nineteenth century.

Paste Term used for porcelain bodies.

Paté dure See *Hard paste*.

Paté tendre See *Hard paste*.

Pipe clay A white firing clay found in small seams with other dark firing secondary clays. It is relatively non plastic. It was used for white inlay of tiles in mediaeval times and until recently was used for press moulded clay pipes for smoking.

Pug mill Machine for pugging clay – mixing it and de-airing it.

Queen's ware A hard earthenware, whiter than the contemporary creamware, with which Josiah Wedgwood had great success and royal patronage.

Raw glaze The term has two distinct meanings; it can mean a glaze made of natural (raw) materials which have not been fritted (such as litharge) or it can mean a glaze applied to an unfired pot.

Ribs Throwers' tools for finishing the surface of pots.

Shale Clay found in deep seams that have been under great pressure, often found adjacent to coal. Shales are usually dark in colour and usually need grinding up before they can be used. Some fireclays occur as shales.

Smoking The slow pre-heating of a biscuit kiln, to allow water vapour to escape. The 'smoking' is, of course, in fact steam.

Soaking The maintenance of a steady heat to allow bodies and glazes time to mature. Ideally no increase or drop in temperature should occur during soaking.

Soft paste See *Hard paste*.

Stack To pack a kiln.

Tea dust See *Hare's Fur*.

Tenmoku A Japanese word for a lustrous, dark iron stoneware glaze. The term covers those black stoneware glazes which break to a warm red brown where thin.

Terra cotta (Literally *burnt earth*). The term is generally applied to unglazed objects made of iron-bearing clays, e.g. terra cotta portraits, terra cotta plant pots.

Tests Are small samples of clay, slip, colour, or glaze etc. fired to discover the colour, texture, etc. of the material or to check the mixing of a newly made batch of clay, slip, colour or glaze etc. As clay is less destructible than notebooks, tests should be clearly marked with relevant details. If the clay tests are lost, notes are not much use but if a notebook is lost and tests are numbered perhaps but not marked with details the tests are frustrating as well as useless.

Top-hat kiln A kiln which can be raised bodily from its base. Work is packed on the base and the kiln is lowered over it. This type of kiln always requires a hoist to raise it and is perhaps most sensibly used if the hoist can travel along an overhead rail to allow the kiln to be used on two or more bases.

Trolley kiln A kiln into which work may be placed on a movable trolley. Trolley kilns can be either intermittent or continuous.

Tunnel kiln A kiln through which trolleys may move allowing a continuous firing of ware to take place. Somewhere near the middle is the hottest part of a tunnel kiln; the work enters the kiln cold and is slowly moved through as fired trolleys are removed from one end and unfired are inserted at the other. A tunnel kiln is termed a continuous kiln.

Water glass Common name for sodium silicate. See *deflocculent*.

Wad box A machine for extruding clay. See *Extrusion*.

FURTHER READING

Books about processes

STONEWARE AND PORCELAIN: THE ART OF HIGH-FIRED POTTERY, Daniel Rhodes, USA, 1959 (First published in Britain 1960)

A POTTER'S BOOK, Bernard Leach, Faber 1940

KILNS: DESIGN, CONSTRUCTION AND OPERATION, Daniel Rhodes, Pitman 1969

PIONEER POTTERY, Michael Cardew, Longmans 1969

DICTIONARY OF CERAMICS, A E Dodd, Newnes 1964

PRACTICAL POTTERY AND CERAMICS, Kenneth Clark, Studio Books 1964

POTTERY: MATERIALS AND TECHNIQUES, David Green, Faber 1967

POTTERY: THE TECHNIQUE OF THROWING, John Colbeck, Batsford 1969: Watson-Guptill USA 1971

KILNS AND KILN FIRING FOR THE CRAFT POTTER, H Fraser, Pitman 1969

ELECTRIC KILNS, H Fraser, Watson-Guptill 1974

Technical books about clay, glaze, glaze formulae and calculations, colours, recipes, etc

FORMULARIO Y PRACTICAS DE CERAMICA, José Llorens Artigas, Editorial Gustavo Gili, SA 1947 (Printed only in Spanish)

CERAMIC COLOURS AND POTTERY DECORATION, Kenneth Shaw, Maclaren 1962

UNDERSTANDING POTTERY GLAZES, David Green, Faber 1963: Watson-Guptill Publications USA 1963

CERAMICS: A POTTER'S HANDBOOK, Glenn C Nelson, Holt, Rinehart and Winston USA 1971

CLAY AND GLAZES FOR THE POTTER, Daniel Rhodes, Pitman 1957, USA (First published in Britain 1969. Revised edition by Chilton, USA 1973)

CERAMIC GLAZES, C W Parmelee, Industrial Publications Inc, Chicago, Illinois, USA 1951

Historical books

POTTERY IN BRITAIN TODAY, Michael Casson, Tiranti 1967

THE ART OF THE MODERN POTTER, Tony Birks, Country Life 1967

THE FABER MONOGRAPHS, fully illustrated and written by specialists on all the main historical types of pottery, Faber

WORLD CERAMICS: AN ILLUSTRATED HISTORY edited by Robert J. Charleston, Hamlyn 1968 (This book contains a very comprehensive reading list.)

SOME USEFUL ADDRESSES

The general suppliers listed below produce full catalogues and supply a very extensive range of materials and equipment. For more specialised needs it is worth also contacting the appropriate specialised suppliers listed subsequently to make comparisons of type, specification or price.

General suppliers

Fulham Pottery Ltd,
210 New Kings Road
London SW6
Tel 01-736-1188

Wengers Ltd
Etruria
Stoke-on-Trent
Staffordshire ST4 7BQ
Tel 0782-25126·
(Stoke-on-Trent exchange)

Podmore and Sons Ltd
Shelton
Stoke-on-Trent
Staffordshire
Tel 0782-24571

Harrison-Mayer Ltd
Meir
Stoke-on-Trent
Staffordshire ST3 7PX
Tel 0782-36111

Kiln suppliers

Cromartie Kilns Ltd
Park Hall Road
Longton Stoke-on-Trent
Staffordshire
Tel 0782-33947

Kilns and Furnaces Ltd
Keele Street Works
Tunstall
Stoke-on-Trent
Staffordshire
Tel 0782-84642

Catterson-Smith Ltd
Adams Bridge Works
South Way
Exhibition Grounds
Wembley
Middlesex HA9 0HN
Tel 01-902-4291

Laboratory and
Research Furnace Co Ltd
Railway Street
Bridgeworth
Shropshire
Tel Ironbridge 3158

Kasenit Ltd
Denbigh Road
Bletchley Bucks
Tel Bletchley 2968

Dawson and Mason Ltd
Alma Works
Levenhulme
Manchester 19
Tel 061-432-0222
(Manchester exchange)

Burner suppliers for oil kilns

Auto Combustions (London) Ltd
360–364 Wandsworth Road
London SW8
Tel 01-622-9121

David Etchells (Furnaces) Ltd
Stafford Road
Darlaston
South Staffordshire
Tel 021-526-2461

Suppliers of refractory and insulating bricks

Moler Products Ltd
Hythe Works
Colchester
Essex
Tel Colchester 73191

Gibbons Refractories Ltd
PO Box 19
Dudley
Worcestershire DY3 2AQ
Tel 0384 55141
(Dudley exchange)

Kiln furniture suppliers

Acme Marls Ltd
Clough Street
Hanley
Stoke-on-Trent
Staffordshire
Tel 0782-2154/2/3

Spray guns: spray booths, etc

The Devilbiss Co Ltd
45 Holborn Viaduct
London EC1
Tel 01-583-4361

Heavy machinery manufacturers: pug mills; lathes; tiles presses; blungers, etc

William Boulton Ltd
Burslem
Stoke-on-Trent
Staffordshire
Tel 0782-88661

Gosling and Gatensbury Ltd
Atlas Works
College Road
Hanley
Stoke-on-Trent
Staffordshire
Tel 0782-22786

Edwards and Jones Ltd
Globe Engineering Works
Longton Stoke-on-Trent
Staffordshire
Tel 0782-33077

Clay suppliers

Potclays Ltd
Brickkiln Lane
Etruria
Stoke-on-Trent
Staffordshire
Tel 0782-29816

Watts, Blake and Bearne
Park House
Courtney Park
Newton Abbot
Devon
Tel Newton Abbot 2345

Moira Pottery Co Ltd
Moira
Near Burton-on-Trent
Leicestershire
Tel 028389 7961
(Swadlincote exchange)

English China Clay Co
John Keay House
St Austell
Cornwall
Tel St Austell 4482

Mellor Mineral Mills Ltd
Etruria Vale
Stoke-on-Trent
Staffordshire
Tel 0782 23441

Glazes, colours, enamels, covercoats, lustres, gold and platinum

Blythe Colours Ltd
Cresswell
Stoke-on-Trent
Staffordshire

Gold and platinum, covercoat for gold and platinum

Hanovia Ltd
Engelhard Industries
Valley Road
Cinderford
Gloucestershire
Tel 0594 22181
(Cinderford exchange)

Screen printing equipment and material suppliers

Screen Process Supplies Ltd
Sericol Group
24 Parsons Green Lane
London SW6
Tel 01-736-8181

E T Marler Ltd
191 Western Road
Merton Abbey
London SW19
Tel 01-640-2211

Transfer paper (Thermaflat Decalcomania)

Brittains Ltd
Cheddleton Paper Mills
Leek
Staffordshire
Tel Leek 360372

Brushes, and specialised materials and tools

E W Good & Co Ltd
Barker Street
Longton
Stoke-on-Trent
Staffordshire
Tel 0782 33460

Asbestos throwing bats

Bingley Son and Follit Ltd
Millbank Works
Minerva Road
London NW10
Tel 01-965-4631

Wheels

Judson and Hudson Ltd
Parker Street Works
Keighley
Yorkshire
Tel 05352-2016
(Keighley exchange)

Woodley's Joinery Works Ltd
(Makers of Leach kick wheels)
Newton Poppleford
Devon
Tel 03956 666
(Colaton Raleigh exchange)

Polythene bottles

Fisons Scientific Apparatus Ltd
Bishops Meadow Road
Loughborough
Leicestershire
Tel Loughborough 5781

Polythene rolls, sheets and bags

Transatlantic Plastics Ltd
29 Victoria Road
Surbiton
Surrey
Tel 01-399-5271
(and many branches)

Books and some tools

Alec Tiranti
72 Charlotte Street
London W1
Tel 01-636-8565

Books

K R Drummond
30 Hart Grove
Ealing Common
London W5
Tel 01-992-1974

Various Refractories

Diamond Clay Company
Stoke Old Clay
Hartshill
Stoke-on-Trent
Staffordshire
Tel 0782 617881
(Newcastle under Lyme exchange)
(also supply Saggar marls coarse clays suitable for large scale handbuilding)

Morgan Refractories
Neston
Wirral
Cheshire L64 3RE
Tel 051-336-3911
(also supply 'T' material, a very refractory white body)

Scale balance and weight suppliers

W & T Avery Ltd (and branches)
Avery House
Clerkenwell Green
London EC1
Tel 01-253-4301

C Morgan & Sons
18 Camden High Street
London NW1
Tel 01-387-2060

A Gallenkamp & Co Ltd
PO Box 290
Technico House
Christopher Street
London EC2
Tel 01-247-3211

USA

General suppliers

Stewart Clay Co Inc
133 Mulberry Street
New York, NY 10013

Jack D Wolfe Co Inc
Brooklyn, NY

Sculpture House Inc
38 East 30 Street
New York, NY 10016

Newton Potter's Supply Inc
96 Rumford Avenue
West Newton, Mass 02165

Duncan Ceramic Products Inc
PO Box 7827
Fresno, California 93727

Bell Ceramics Inc
Box 697 Clermont, Florida 32711

Throwing wheels

Gilmour Campbell
14258 Maiden
Detroit, Michigan 48213

Randall Wheel
Box 531 Alfred, NY

J T Abernathy
212 South State Street
Ann Abor, Michigan

Paul Soldner
Aspen, Colorado

Advanced Kiln Co
2543 Whittier Boulevard
Los Angeles, California

A.D. Alpine Inc
11837 Teale Street
Culver City, California

Skutt and Son
Box 202
Olympia, Washington

Kilns

Unique Kilns
530 Spruce Street
Trenton, New Jersey

Dickinson Kilns Inc
2424 Glover Place
Los Angeles, California

Denver Fire Clay Co
3033 Black Street
Denver, Colorado

Pereny Equipment Co Inc
Dept CD, 893 Chambers Road
Columbus, Ohio 43211

Clays

Edgar Plastic Kaolin Co
Edgar, Putnam County, Florida

A P Green Refractories Co
1018 East Breckenridge Street
Mexico, Missouri 65265

George Fetzer Co
1205 17th Avenue
Columbus, Ohio 43211

Kentucky-Tennessee Clay Co Inc
Box 447, Mayfield,
Kentucky 42066

Bell Clay Co
Gleason, Tennessee 38229

Harris Clay Co
Box 429
Spruce Pine,
North Carolina 28777

Cedar Heights Clay Co
50 Portsmouth Road
Oak Hill, Ohio 45656

Georgia Kaolin Co
433 North Broad Street
Elizabeth, New Jersey 07207

Other equipment

Simpson Mix-Muller Division
National Engineering Co
Suite 2060,
20 North Wacker Street
Chicago, Illinois 60606

Amaco
(American Art Clay Company)
4717 West 16th Street
Indianapolis, Indiana 46222

Patterson-Ludlow Division
Banner Industries Ltd
1250 Saint George Street
East Liverpool, Ohio 43920

J C Steele and Sons Co
710 South Mulberry Street
Drawer 951
Statesville, North Carolina 28677

Jamar Walker Corp Inc
365 South First Avenue
East Duluth, Minnesota 55802

Ohaus
29 Hanover Road, Florham Park
New Jersey 07932

Brodhead-Garrett Co
4560 East 71st Street
Cleveland, Ohio 44105

Notes for American readers

Terms

Cornish stone from Cornwall, England
polythene – polythylene
Asbestolux – asbestos mill board
lino – linoleum
soft soap – *Ivory*

Centigrade	*Fahrenheit*
100°	212°
130°	266°
200°	392°
700°	1292°
900°	1652°
1000°	1832°
1050°	1922°
1100°	2012°
1150°	2102°
1250°	2282°
1300°	2372°

Metric	*Imperial*
6 mm	$\frac{1}{4}$ in.
25 mm	1 in.
29 mm	$1\frac{1}{8}$ in.
38 mm	$1\frac{1}{2}$ in.
50 mm	2 in.
64 mm	$2\frac{1}{2}$ in.
76 mm	3 in.
102 mm	4 in.
122 cm × 46 cm	4 ft × 18 in.

Index

Soda ash 78 117